THE
MIGHTY EIGHTH
IN
COLOUR

THE MIGHTY EIGHTH
IN
COLOUR

ROGER A. FREEMAN

ARMS AND
ARMOUR

Arms and Armour Press
A Cassell Imprint
Villiers House, 41–47 Strand,
London WC2N 5JE

Distributed in Australia by
Capricorn Link (Australia) Pty.
Ltd, P.O. Box 665, Lane Cove,
New South Wales 2066

*British Library Cataloguing in
Publication Data*
Freeman, Roger A. (Roger
Anthony), *1928–*
The mighty eighth in colour.
I. Title
940.544973

ISBN 1-85409-095-X

Edited and designed by Roger
Chesneau
Typeset by Typesetters
(Birmingham) Ltd and
Ronset Typesetting Ltd
Printed and bound in Singapore

Half-title page illustration:
Lt Col Francis S. Gabreski posing
in the cockpit of his Thunderbolt a
few days before he had to crash-
land in enemy-held territory. With
28 confirmed victories, 'Gabby'
Gabreski was the top-scoring
USAAF fighter pilot flying against
the *Luftwaffe* and he was credited
with an additional 5½ aircraft
destroyed in the Korean War.
(USAF K2170)

Title-page illustration:
Two clipped-wing Spitfire VBs
used for transitional training from
F-5s to Spitfire XIs, at Mount
Farm. (Robert Astrella)

Below: *Alice Blue Gown* (790 BG),
up from Eye, sails above an
undercast with her lethal cargo.
(Arnold N. Delmonico)

ACKNOWLEDGEMENTS
Collecting the colour material reproduced in this volume entailed a
prodigious amount of communication with veterans and others. In
many instances, transparencies obtained in the war years had remained
among the owner's memorabilia, rarely reviewed and occasionally even
forgotten. Locating and selecting the photographs depended largely on
the generosity of many individuals who supplied the required material
and gave permission for its use. Others sought out colour photographs
in various archives, going to considerable trouble to secure specific
subjects for the compiler. I am indebted to them all, and my expression
of grateful thanks is sincere but, in the circumstances, seems
inadequate.

Contributors and helpers were: Trevor Allen, Constant Anszperger,
Paul Andrews, Robert Andrews, Lou Ades, John Archer, Robert
Astrella, Michael Bailey, Ralph Ballinger, Mason Barnard, Steve
Birdsall, Cliff Bishop, Tim Bivens, Mrs Nelloise Blue, Tom Britton,
Alfo Brusetti, Walter Byrne, Robert Cavanagh, C. H. Bud Chamber-
lain, William Charles, Tom Cooper, Paul Chryst, Alan Crouchman,
Arnold Delmonico, Johnny Driscoll, Richard DeBruin, Jeff Ethell,
Aldon Ferguson, Bruce Finch, Douglas Fisher, Arthur Fitch, Garry
Fry, William Furniss, Robert Foose, Charles Freudenthal, Royal Frey,
Michael Gibson, Frank Gyidik, Amos Golisch, Chris Gotts, Steve
Gotts, Jim Goar, Cliff Hall, Clint Hammond, Don Hanson, Vince
Hemmings, Harry Holmes, Ed Huntzinger, Jack Ilfrey, John R.
Johnson, Herbert Kaster, Al Keeler, John Kirkwood, David Knight,
Albert Krassman, John Kreidler, Robert Kuhnert, Chester Klier,
George Letlow, Eli Levine, Leo Lester, Morton Luman, Edmund
Lutz, Dan McGovern, Ian McLachlan, Norman Malayney, Steven D.
Miller, Kent Miller, Robert B. Miller, Danny Morris, Wiley Noble,
Fred Nowosad, Merle Olmsted, Dave Osborne, Allen Ostrom, George
Parker, Leslie Peterson, Jack Phegley, Robert Powell, Irwin Pochter,
Ed Richie, Clark Rollins Jr, Herb Rutland, Robert Sand, Roland Scott,
James D. Smith, Russell Strong, Robert Sturges, Sam Sox Jr, Harry
Task, Warren Stanley, Glenn Tessmer, Frank Thomas, Byron E.
Trent, Robert Waltz, Geoff Ward, Richard L. Ward, Bob Welty, Ted
Wurm, John Wilson, Jim Young and, last but not least, the ever
helpful members of the 100th Bomb Group Memorial Museum.

Generous help was forthcoming from archives, namely the Air Force
Museum at Dayton, the Library of Congress and the National Air and
Space Museum in Washington. In particular, the Air Force Academy,
through the good offices of Duane J. Reed, made a major contribution.

On the production side, Patricia Keen did stalwart work as the
compiler's assistant; Norman Ottaway produced the location map;
Bruce Robertson cast an eye over editorial matters; and Jean Freeman,
together with Alice Apricot, produced the manuscripts. Ian Mactaggart
deserves special mention as many of the pictures in this volume are as a
result of his photographic expertise with original material. To all, my
heartfelt thanks.

Roger A. Freeman

CONTENTS

INTRODUCTION

COLOUR IS NOW the common form of photography, with monochrome the exception. The reverse was the case until the 1950s, when colour film became generally available at acceptable cost. Although a process for colour photography had been developed in France in 1907 and others were devised during the following two decades, all were both expensive and complicated. Then, in 1935, the American Kodak company marketed Kodachrome, which provided the means of good quality and, eventually, reasonably priced colour photography. However, this involved positive images on film, and it was not until 1942 that Kodak produced a negative-print process, and this, with refinement and lower cost, would only find general use several years later. In Britain during 1932 the Frenchman M. Dufay joined with Spicers, the paper manufacturers, to produce colour film and by 1938 Dufaycolor was being marketed with full processing facilities. Although its acceptance by the cinema was limited, it was popular with amateurs as processing was simple, but production ceased early in the war when the firm was directed to government work. Agfa, the German manufacturer, announced a colour negative-print method in 1936 but its development, and the Second World War, delayed general marketing until 1949.

At the time of the United States' entry into the Second World War, in December 1941, Kodachrome was still something of a novelty. The company marketed colour film for popular cameras in selected sizes, the most common and economical being 35mm width, which was simply short lengths of stock similar to that used by the American movie industry. A 35mm frame could be installed in a mount and viewed through an illuminated enlarger, various models of which were produced to meet a growing demand. However, development of the exposed film had to be carried out by special Kodak laboratories and the overall expense made colour photography very much a luxury.

The Kodak subsidiary in the United Kingdom had the means for limited processing of Kodachrome in 1939 but its film stock had to be imported from the United States and none was forthcoming during the war years. Colour film in British hands between 1939 and 1945 was either old Dufaycolor stock or brought to the UK privately by individuals – or it was obtained by government or military bodies for special purposes. Indeed, the British public was soon denied even normal monochrome film from home production, which went to the Services or for uses decreed by government departments.

When US forces were sent to Europe in 1942 they were permitted to take personal cameras, and although the taking of photographs at military establishments was forbidden this regulation was not rigidly observed. Parents sent Kodachrome reels to serving sons and daughters both as unsolicited gifts and on request. Even so, colour film remained comparatively rare in GIs' cameras, and it

▲ Contrails streaming behind a B-17F formation at 28,000 feet en route to Villacoublay, 14 July 1943. This picture was taken by T/Sgt Dan McGovern from the radio room hatch of *Moonbeam McSwain*, a 365th BS, 305th BG aircraft coded 'XK:Y'. (Daniel A. McGovern)

◄ Eye airfield from the air, looking due north. At the bottom right-hand corner of the bomb store area, part of the Yaxley–Diss road can be seen. No 1 hangar and the main technical site are at top left. The three intersecting runways, common to all wartime airfields built to Class 'A' standard for bomber operation, were identified by compass degrees relative to the direction of approach. The 6,000-foot long main runway positioned SSW to NNE was runway 03 from this direction and 21 when approached from the other. (Mark Brown: Air Force Academy)

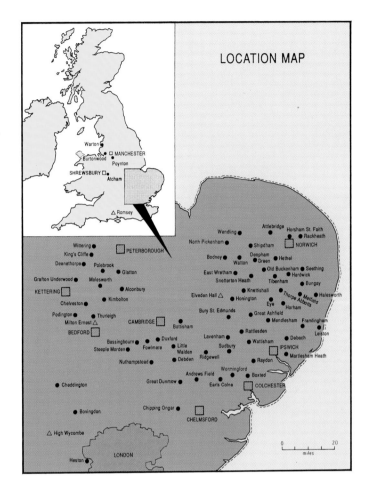

LOCATION MAP

▲ Smart and ready to hit town. US officers had four different uniforms and one of the most popular was based around the 'Ike' jacket, so called because of General Eisenhower's frequent use of it. Although similarly clad, Lt Lucius Ades and Lt Preston G. Redd, pilot and navigator of the same pathfinder crew, have a different choice of tie. Note also that Redd has the blue Distinguished Unit Citation ribbon above his right breast pocket and that for the Air Medal above the left. Both hats have been squashed out of the original shape – the mark of the combat flier. The photograph was taken on the 567th Bomb Squadron living site. (Lucius R. Ades)

▼ A 63rd Fighter Squadron armourer, working on a .50-inch calibre Browning machine gun and using a 350-round ammunition box as a bench. The eight guns of a Thunderbolt had to be stripped and cleaned regularly to ensure that they would function properly and this task took, on average, around two hours. This photograph was taken at Boxted, facing north near the wooded area concealing the bomb and ammunition stores. (Mark Brown: Air Force Academy)

would appear that in some units no one ever wielded a camera loaded with Kodachrome. Those who did 'shoot color' usually sent the exposed film to Kodak in London for processing, but this was a slow service and one at times hindered by censorship.

A limited number of transparencies were taken by official military photographers and these were usually of much better quality than those produced by amateurs. Nevertheless, many hobby photographers in the USAAF did outstanding work, despite the handicap of the simple lens installed in the 'popular' cameras of those days. Individuals took these pictures for no other reasons than the novelty and pleasure of recording scenes which, particularly where aircraft were concerned, were highly colourful. Indeed, the spectacle that the massive Second World War operations of the 8th Air Force provided is probably without equal, both in the sky and on airfields. Individuals rated the resulting slides as souvenirs of their service, probably without thought of any historical significance that this material might one day possess.

Faced with the knowledge that colour photography was comparatively rare during the Second World War, it was necessary for the compiler to advertise his objectives when setting out to produce this photographic presentation. The response was remarkable, allowing reasonable coverage of the 8th Air Force in Europe and including most of the major bases. Nevertheless, colour photographs of a number of bases simply could not be traced, and in consequence, relevant units cannot be represented. If some reproductions are not

A SELECTION OF 8TH AIR FORCE UNIT INSIGNIA

303rd Bomb Group

392nd Bomb Group

364th Bomb Squadron

365th Bomb Squadron

366th Bomb Squadron

557th Bomb Squadron

559th Bomb Squadron

615th Bomb Squadron

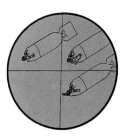

700th Bomb Squadron

702nd Bomb Squadron

703rd Bomb Squadron

714th Bomb Squadron

715th Bomb Squadron

359th Fighter Group

350th Fighter Squadron

351st Fighter Squadron

352nd Fighter Squadron

434th Fighter Squadron

435th Fighter Squadron

436th Fighter Squadron

► Taking advantage of off-duty time on a warm July day, Pfc Robert Mackay gets his hair cut by S/Sgt Robert Buck while Sgt William Kinsey looks on. Such days were rare, but it could be warm in England. (Wallace A. Portouw)

to the standard expected today, the limitations of the original colour process, of the cameras and of the amateur operators should be considered, together with the fact that the original transparencies have suffered half a century's abrasion and light erosion.

There was a natural tendency for the individual serviceman to select colourful subjects to capture on Kodachrome. Aircraft paintwork was a frequent attraction, as the large number of pictures devoted to aircraft in this volume indicate. The English countryside was probably the next most popular subject and one's 'buddies' the third. In presenting these photographs the compiler has endeavoured to give as much information as practicable about what is depicted and, whenever possible, to state the precise location at which the picture was taken.

Some reproductions have been taken from 16mm and 8mm footage; photographers often obtained the former from date-expired, unexposed gun-camera cassettes while the latter was sent or brought from the US where it could be purchased for 'home movies'. With both 16mm and 8mm, definition varies considerably but is rarely as sharp as in the 35mm originals. In asking acceptance of these poorer quality photographs, the compiler again reminds the reader of the rarity of colour photographs during the war years.

The arrangement of these colour photographs is by base, presented alphabetically, giving coverage to the units serving at that location as far as the material has allowed. Aircraft photographed at locations other than their home base are, as a general rule, presented under their home station.

▼ When returning from a mission it was policy to reduce altitude and spread formations to ease the aircrew's lot: here, showing signs of wear and with a replacement left outer wing panel salvaged from a wrecked Fortress, *Miss Bea Haven* heads for home. The gun in the radio operator's position had been discarded by this date (26 August 1944). Shadows of the formation's aircraft can be seen on the harvest fields below. The photograph was taken from the nose, over the gun operating arm; the gun handle is in the right-hand corner. (Mark Brown: Air Force Academy)

▼ All told, 158 airfields were allocated at one time or another for 8th Air Force use and of these 122 actually had some USAAF presence. The plan called for 75 bomber airfields built to Class A standard, which provided for one main and two auxiliary hard-surfaced runways with perimeter track and hardstandings for 50 aircraft. The standard also required a comprehensive technical site with two large maintenance hangars, workshops and fuel stores for 72,000 gallons, accommodation

for 3,000 personnel and services independent of the local water, sewage and electricity supplies. Alconbury, one of the early bomber airfields opened in 1942, was enlarged that winter and the following year. Here the north-east corner of the airfield is viewed from the top turret of an orbiting B-17, May 1943. Runway 12-30 is in the distance and hardstanding No 18 is in the left foreground with a 92nd Bomb Group B-17 in residence. The airfield was still being expanded at this date and other

hardstandings were later added in this area. (USAAF)

▼ Airfield dispersal points – hardstands or hardstandings on Class A airfields – were often close to villages and farms. This B-17F of the 92nd Bomb Group parked on hardstand No 29 is not far from the centre of Little Stukeley, whose church tower was a familiar landmark to airmen using Alconbury. (USAAF)

ALCONBURY

482 BG
812/813/814 BS

▼ Many of the colour photographs in the following pages reflect bright and often amusing aspects of the 8th Air Force, tending to conceal the death and destruction that was a

frequent experience. Flying itself was fraught with danger, apart from combat. For every six aircraft missing in action one was lost through a non-operational accident.

One of the most horrific accidents occurred at Brome, Suffolk, at approximately 10.30 in the morning of 10 November 1943. It involved the first B-17F Fortress fitted with H2S ground-scanning radar for use in locating targets through cloud. The aircraft, 42-5793, 'PC:M' of the 813th Bomb Squadron, had been sent from Alconbury to Thorpe Abbotts to fly with the 100th Bomb Group, which was scheduled to lead an air task force that day. As poor weather caused the mission to be cancelled, this 482nd Group pathfinder Fortress took off in a south-westerly direction to return to its home base. No sooner had the aircraft become airborne, however, than an engine caught fire.

The pilot apparently tried to crash-land on the newly

constructed runway at Eye, almost dead ahead, but the aircraft hit the ground some 300 yards short, smashed across the road and was immediately engulfed in flames. Of four County Council employees working on the road at this point with a horse and cart, two were killed outright and two injured, one so badly that he died shortly after being admitted to hospital. The horse was also killed. None of the aircraft's thirteen occupants, who included two radar mechanics, escaped the inferno which resulted from the ignition of incendiary bombs it was carrying and little was left of the aircraft except the fire-scorched tail fin. The shoe on a dismembered horse leg can be seen at the bottom left-hand corner of the photograph. (100th BG Memorial Museum)

▶ 'Tired' fighters were moved to training establishments. This P-47C, 41-6530 'VM:A' of the 551st Fighter Training Squadron, provided operational training for pilots received from US training establishments and was often the 'mount' of the CO at Atcham. It bears the standard white Thunderbolt type-recognition markings, spring 1944. (Robert Astrella)

▼ *Kokomo* was the personal Thunderbolt 'acquired' by Maj. Gen. William Kepner, commanding VIII Fighter Command, from the 495th Fighter Group. This distinctive green-nosed P-47D moved home base from Atcham to Bovingdon and then, when Bill Kepner took command of the 2nd Division, it went to Hethel. While the general, a First World War fighter pilot, was officially not permitted to fly over enemy-held territory, he was known to have ventured close in the course of monitoring his forces in the air. The picture was taken at Mount Farm, autumn 1944. (Robert Astrella)

► Hydraulic failures due to damage sustained during combat missions presented pilots with landing difficulties. Landing gear and flap lowering could be operated by emergency systems but not the wheel brakes, without which a B-17 or B-24 might require more than a mile to come to a stop. As there was usually less than three-quarters of a mile of runway left after touch-

down, the result was either a ground loop or overrun. A technique for checking aircraft speed, if brakes were inoperative, was simultaneously to release a parachute from the waist window on each side of the bomber's fuselage. The parachutes, anchored to gun mounts, were fed out as soon as the main wheels touched the runway. A demonstration of this

technique is being carried out on *Pegasus, the Flying Red Horse*, a Pathfinder B-24J of the 784th Bomb Squadron. This aircraft carried a retractable H2X radar scanner in the well originally used to site the under turret. *Pegasus* served with the 466th BG from July 1944 until the end of hostilities. (USAAF K2334A)

◄ Sheet metal men repairing a tail fin for use as a replacement when needed. The donor Liberator was *The Mad Monk*, which was written off in a crash-landing at Swanton Morley having hit tree-tops after taking off from home base. (USAAF)

▶ The Liberator used by the 466th Bomb Group for formation assembly purposes had a combat career with the 93rd Bomb Group at Hardwick before retirement. Named *Ready and Willing*, it had taken part in the famous low-level mission to the Ploesti oil refineries in Romania, flown by John Roche's crew. Applying the distinctive markings to this aircraft at Attlebridge after the original camouflage paint had been removed proved to be a very demanding task. The large letter 'L' on the white vertical tail was the group identity letter. The aircraft was photographed on hardstand number 52, near Weston Green, looking north-west (George Parker)

► The main camp and south side of the airfield from the air, summer 1944. Bassingbourn was originally constructed in 1938 and its good barracks and other amenities made it a favoured station for USAAF personnel. To accommodate a heavy bomber group, the runways were lengthened and an extensive network of taxiways with hardstands was constructed in 1942; those seen in the top right corner were used by the 401st Bomb Squadron. To the left of the airfield is the A10 London–Cambridge highway, an old Roman road. A UC-64 Norseman utility aircraft can be seen on runway 17 and several B-17s are parked in front of the hangar apron. (USAAF Bassingbourn Tower Museum)

▲ An airman who regularly took his camera loaded with colour film on combat missions was 1/Lt Paul Chryst of the 401st Bomb Squadron. Here B-17s of the 91st Group are on course to the target at Brandenburg, 6 August 1944, with a barrage of flak – more than 60 bursts – slightly early and to the left. The 91st returned from this 9½-hour mission with no aircraft lost; the other groups briefed for this target were not so fortunate and lost eleven. (Paul Chryst)

► A B-17 that has wandered to the right of the formation on the bomb run passes 'the point', where the Lead and Deputy Lead bombers release their loads and twin white smoke markers which quickly disperse into weird shapes in the cold blue sky. (Paul Chryst)

▲ The formation heads for home after bombing. Smoke marker target indicators dropped by the next attacking formation can be seen in the distance. The B-17G named *Hey Daddy* flew with the 91st from late July 1944 to survive and return to the US a year later. (Paul Chryst)

▲ Harry Garner's crew disembarked from another mission. Lt Paul Chryst, reaching into the right gun opening of the chin turret, is recovering a piece of German flak for a souvenir. *Times A-Wastin* was lost to flak with Lt Peter Pastre's crew on its 107th mission, 8 April 1945. (Paul Chryst)

▼ *Yankee Doddle* was the 97th Bomb Group B-17E in which Gen. Eaker, Commanding General of VIII Bomber Command, flew on the very first 8th Air Force heavy

bomber mission, 17 August 1942. By the summer of 1944 (when photographed at Bodney) the aircraft, a 'hack' for the 91st Bomb Group, was used as a liaison transport. The original framed nosepiece of this B-17E model has been replaced by one from an F model. The insignia is that of the 323rd Bomb Squadron. (Robert Bruner)

▲ Suggestive decor on *Mount 'N Ride* of the 323rd Bomb Squadron painted by Sgt Tony Stracer, who was responsible for most of the artwork requested by members of this unit. On 16 March 1944 this B-17G suffered damage and limped into neutral Switzerland where it remained for the duration. (Paul Chryst)

▼ In July 1944 the 1st Combat Bomb Wing was the first B-17-equipped organization to introduce bright identity markings for formation recognition on the

aircraft of its three groups. The spray painter and the man with the brush appear to be using two different shades of red to adorn the fin of the 324th Bomb Squadron's *Little Miss Mischief*. (USAAF)

◄ *Nine O Nine* set a record for 8th Air Force Fortresses in completing 140 combat missions without once having had to turn back for mechanical reasons. Here M/Sgt Rollin L. Davis, the crew chief, touches up the 120th raid symbol for the photographer on a cold February day in 1945. The location was hardstand D5 in the 323rd Bomb Squadron dispersal area, which was reached by crossing the A14 Royston–Huntingdon road, the Ermine Street of Roman times. This dispersal area was built in the elm-lined avenue that ran towards Wimpole Hall. (USAAF)

BASSINGBOURN

1 SF

857 BS

► A red spinner, white noseband and red edging to the tail surfaces were the identity markings adopted by the 1st Scouting Force for its Mustangs. The first of the scouting units, tasked with preceding bomber formations to their target area to report on local weather, the 1st SF operated from Honington until March 1945, when the unit was given squadron status and moved to Bassingbourn. P-51D '9H:L' was photographed on a visit to Thurleigh in early May 1945. (Ben Marcilonis)

▼ Capt. Stephen W. Andrew taxies out to take off in his P-47D *Prairie Farmer* after a visit to Wittering in October 1943. This Thunderbolt was transferred to the 9th Air Force after the 352nd Fighter Group converted to Mustangs; it went missing in action with the 373rd Fighter Group on 24 May 1944.

Seven months later, as a major, Andrew led the 486th Fighter Squadron on the first 'shuttle' escort mission to Russia but had to bale out over Hungary on 2 July when his P-51's engine failed. He was credited with eight air victories and seven through strafing, plus another air victory obtained during

previous service in the South-West Pacific. (Air Force Museum)

▼ Lt Col. John C. Edwards of the 352nd FG Headquarters and the ground crew who maintained his personal P-51D *Barbara M. 4th*, about spring 1945. The Mustang was named after Edwards' wife. The jettisonable fuel tanks on the wing pylons were the 75 US gallon capacity type. (Joe Sabanos)

▼ One of the longest serving Mustangs at Bodney, *Snoot's Sniper* was there for over a year, having been classified War Weary long before VE-Day. The crew chief for its combat service was S/Sgt Arthur Snyder. The original pilot assigned to this aircraft was Lt Francis

Horne, credited with destroying 5½ enemy aircraft in air combat. (Robert Astrella)

► Capt. Richard J. DeBruin, 352nd FG Maintenance and Supply Officer, makes a 'rigid digit' sign in front of the Bugs Bunny insignia on a 328th Fighter Squadron P-47D, March 1944. The aircraft, which carried the slogan *Slender, Tender and Tall*, was assigned to Capt. William T. Halton, Operations Officer of the squadron. By the end of hostilities Bill Halton was credited with destroying 10½ enemy aircraft in the air and two others by ground strafing; he also gained the rank of lieutenant colonel. He was killed in action in the Korean War. (Richard J. DeBruin)

▲ Bottisham airfield, looking to the north-east, from the 361st's Fairchild UC-61 utility aircraft, September 1944. The village and church lie beyond the Pierced Steel Plank runway and the main technical area. The barely visible track crossing the runway was an old road which P-51 pilot Jim Smith recalls as 'an interesting bump at take-off speed with full load'. (James D. Smith)

▲ ▶ Col Tom Christian, CO of the 361st, banks his personal Mustang over Cambridgeshire on a July afternoon in 1944. Named after the pilot's wife, *Lou IV* had Insignia Blue paint on much of the upper surfaces to meet the requirement that where possible those fighter types received in natural metal finish should have some camouflage colour applied. The reason was the possibility of VIII Fighter Command units being required to operate from forward airstrips on the Continent which might be more liable to enemy air attack than UK bases. Insignia Blue was only applied to a few aircraft of the 361st at Bottisham, presumably as the supply of a more suitable green was limited at the time. *Lou IV* was also the first P-51 in the 361st to have the Group's identifying yellow nose marking extended well back along the cowling. Col Christian was shot down and killed in this aircraft while engaged in a ground attack on 12 August 1944. (USAAF)

►A flight of 375th Fighter Squadron Mustangs leads a flight of the 376th over an undercast in July 1944. The mixture of P-51B and P-51D models includes several with camouflage paint applied to the upper fuselage decking, wings and tails. (USAAF K2495)

◄*Small Fry IV* and a flight from the 376th Fighter Squadron await the signal to begin take-off, August 1944. At the time this was 1/Lt Jimmie Wright's aircraft until he finished his tour. On 27 September 1/Lt Victor Bocquin claimed three enemy aircraft while flying this P-51 in an air battle near Kassel. (James D. Smith)

▼ A view from the 376th Fighter Squadron dispersals at Little Wilbraham, looking along the eastern perimeter track towards Bottisham village, August 1944. Only the perimeter track and some of the dispersal points were hard-surfaced on the flying field. A formation of 1st Division B-17s can be seen heading for home. (James D. Smith)

◄Resplendent in 'D-Day stripes', the black and white markings specially applied on the eve of the cross-channel invasion to identify 'friendly' aircraft to Allied forces, Mustangs await the take-off signal on a bright June day. Of the 374th Fighter Squadron aircraft in the foreground, *Bald Eagle III* carries some additional yellow and black striping applied by its ground crew so that when this aircraft was among others it was easily distinguishable to them. Other P-51s are of the 376th Fighter Squadron. The photograph was taken at the end of runway 01 (steel mat) looking east towards a blister type hangar.

► The operational training unit set up in 1942 to indoctrinate air crew freshly arrived from the USA in the procedures used by VIII Bomber Command in the UK was originally run by the 92nd Bomb Group and then its 326th Bomb Squadron. The 92nd had inherited the B-17Es of the 97th Bomb Group, the organization that flew VIII Bomber Command's first heavy bomber mission on 17 August 1942. These B-17Es flew out their days on training duties or as 'hack' aircraft for many combat units. This nameless B-17E saw service with the 97th Bomb Group at Polebrook before going to Bovingdon in

September 1942. All its armament had been removed when the aircraft was photographed in summer 1944

but the 326th Bomb Squadron markings were retained. The aircraft later served with the 100th

Bomb Group at Thorpe Abbotts as a staff fly-around. (Robert Astrella)

◄ 'A' Flight of the 8th Air Force Headquarters Squadron held liaison and combat aircraft types at Bovingdon for use by staff officers visiting other locations. The composition varied as the months went past, but at one time it had on strength an AT-6D, an AT-7, a P-38J, a P-39M, a P-40F, a P-47D, an AT-23A, an A-20G, an RDB-7B, two UC-61As, two UC-45Fs and two UC-78s. The RDB-7B was the designation used for a Douglas Boston III, serial AL672, acquired direct from an RAF contract in August 1942. Originally used to equip the 15th Bomb Squadron at Podington, it spent most of its life in communications flights. It was one of only three Bostons retained by the 8th Air Force at the end of hostilities. (Robert Astrella)

► B-17E 41-2578 was the oldest and longest serving Fortress in the 8th Air Force. It was the aircraft in which Col Frank Armstrong led the first heavy bomber mission on 17 August 1942. The name *Butcher Shop* was attributed to it, although there is no known evidence that this was ever painted on the aircraft. This Fortress spent most of its flying time on training and communication duties. When photographed in October 1942 it was assigned to the 92nd Bomb Group at Bovingdon. (USAAF)

▼ A bomb-laden B-26C clears the end of runway 28 and crosses the nearby public road at under 50 feet as it climbs west, August 1943. Marauders used most of such 4,200 feet runways before becoming airborne. (USAAF via C. Klier)

▼ *Winnie* was usually flown by Maj. Charles W. ('Chuck') Lockhart, CO of the 552nd Bomb Squadron. When photographed early in August 1943 this B-26B had completed two diversions (bogus combat missions over the Channel to draw enemy attention from real offensive operations) and two bombing attacks, as indicated by the two yellow duck and two bomb

symbols respectively. The Squadron's official insignia, a winged skull on a bomb, adorns the nosewheel centre cover. (USAAF via C. Klier)

BOXTED

◄ Aircraft, like ships, were usually considered female by those who worked with them, which accounts for the predominance of girls' names and the suggestions of a wayward nature when it came to naming. *Shack Rat* was a P-47D assigned to the 63rd Fighter Squadron, and the 'girly' art underlines the implication. The towing vehicle is a military adaption of a light agricultural tractor. The photograph was taken on a loop hardstand near the bomb dump area, looking north. (Mark Brown: Air Force Academy)

▶ Presenting the famous scarlet noseband that identified the aircraft of one of the most successful US fighter groups, *Belle of Belmont* taxies round the perimeter track carrying two 150 US gallon jettisonable fuel tanks on its wing racks. Aircraft with these tanks full required careful handling, but their tactical radius of action was extended to more than 500 miles from base. In the background can be seen the store of various types of 'drop tank' stacked near Lodge Lane; No 1 hangar is just out of the picture on the right. *Belle of Belmont* was another aircraft received in 'silver' finish but given a green top-coat. (Mark Brown: Air Force Academy)

▶ Col David Schilling, CO of the 56th Fighter Group, in the cockpit of his 'LM:S', ready to roll on runway 28, early September 1944. This was one of the first three Thunderbolts with the so-called 'bubble hood' cockpit cover, received by the 56th and at first dubbed 'Superbolts', that served with the Group until the early spring of the following year. Fifteen victory symbols are painted below the cockpit; a few days after this photograph was taken, Dave Schilling shot down three enemy planes in one day while flying this aircraft. (Mark Brown: Air Force Academy)

◀ Back from a mission, Thunderbolt 'LM:A' is refuelled. The P-47's engine 'drank' 100 US gallons an hour in cruise flight and nearly three times that amount at maximum power (only permissible for very short periods in an emergency). This aircraft has apparently seen action as the guns have been removed from the wings and taken for cleaning. Ammunition boxes have been delivered to replenish wing magazine bays. Lt Wilburn A. Haggard was lost in this aircraft on 18 December 1944 but survived as a prisoner of war. (Mark Brown: Air Force Academy)

▲ The rear elements of the 63rd Fighter Squadron marshalling. The worn Thunderbolt in the foreground, assigned to Lt Cameron M. Hart, wears a motif of a big cat crushing a Nazi fighter in its jaws. Hart was eventually credited with six aerial victories and at this time, September 1944, had claims of two which are recorded on the fuselage below four cross symbols representing the victories credited to the previous 'owner' of 'UN:B', Lt Marvin H. Becker, who had completed his tour of operations. The aircraft went missing with another pilot in November 1944. (Mark Brown: Air Force Academy)

◄◄ Lt Col David Schilling, Air Executive of the 56th Fighter Group at the date of this photograph, in front of his P-47D. A flamboyant and popular character, he was CO of the 62nd Fighter Squadron when the 56th first arrived in the UK and became Group CO when Col Zemke moved to the 479th Fighter Group at Wattisham in August 1944. Dave Schilling was credited with destroying 22½ enemy aircraft in the air and 10½ on the ground before being removed from combat in January 1945. The halves were shared credits. (USAAF)

◄ Col Hubert Zemke, original combat commander of the 56th and one of the most colourful fighter leaders of the Second World War. Maj. Gen. Kepner, Commanding General of VIII Fighter Command, considered Hub Zemke his best group commander. (USAAF)

▲ The Air Sea Rescue Squadron CO's aircraft on a loop dispersal at the back of Park Farm, Langham Moor, where the house served as accommodation and offices for the unit. Formed in May 1944, the Squadron used worn P-47Ds to carry dinghy packs and sea-marker equipment for use in search and rescue work. The unit was distinguished by red, white and blue nose bands and a single yellow stripe over each flight surface. Although this photograph was taken in early September 1944, the Squadron's aircraft retain the temporary 'D-Day stripes' on their upper surfaces. The view is to the north-east, with cottages in Park Lane beyond the uncompleted blister hangar being erected for the ASR unit. (Mark Brown: Air Force Academy)

▼ *Lady Loralie* lands on runway 28. The red patch on the lowered wing flap was a 'No Step' warning. This P-47D, serving in the Air Sea Rescue Squadron from soon after its formation, was lost in a collision with another P-47 of the unit over Fritton Lake, Suffolk, on 8 April 1945. At that time the Squadron was operating from Halesworth as the 5th Emergency Rescue Squadron. (Mark Brown: Air Force Academy)

◄ *Lady Luck*, an original combat B-24H of the 704th Bomb Squadron, displays 49 mission-completed symbols plus a claim for an enemy fighter destroyed. On 15 October 1944, after being shot up by flak, this aircraft managed to land at an airfield in France but the damage was such that it was not repairable. (Albert R. Krassman)

▼ *Lassie Come Home*, of the 707th Bomb Squadron, didn't on 4 November 1944 when it was the only Liberator lost from the force attacking oil targets in north-west Germany. On this occasion it was flown by a 705th Bomb Squadron crew, six of whom were killed. Lassie is shown chasing two Nazis. The aircraft's 'bubble' window was an 'in service' addition to facilitate the navigator's observation of landmarks. (Albert R. Krassman)

▲ *Naughty Nan*, a B-24H of the 705th Bomb Squadron, was landing back from a local flight but only the right undercarriage extended and that jammed down. Forced to make a crash-landing at base, the aircraft was wrecked. (Albert R. Krassman)

► *White Lit'nin'*, a 705th Bomb Squadron B-24H, suffered hydraulic system failure while on a local flight, forcing its pilots to make a wheels-up landing at Woodbridge emergency airfield, where the aircraft was salvaged on 30 March 1945. (Albert R. Krassman)

▼ *Kentucky Belle*, a late model B-24J with inward-retracting nosewheel doors, thermal anti-icing and other innovations, photographed after completing 80 bombing missions, three 'truckings' of gasoline to France and one supply drop. The insignia on the right side of this aircraft was arguably the most eye-catching at Bungay. The bomber had previously served with the 490th Bomb Group at Eye. (Albert R. Krassman)

▼ A starboard view of *Kentucky Belle*, with Albert Krassman posing by the aircraft. (Albert R. Krassman)

◄ Shrapnel damage to the rear fuselage of *Ginger*. This B-24H was one of three 446th Bomb Group Liberators lost on 26 August 1944. Shot down by flak, five of the crew were killed and five made prisoner. The aircraft had begun its combat life as one of the few B-24s of the 482nd Bomb Group equipped with H2S ground-scanning radar for pathfinder work. (Albert R. Krassman)

BURY ST EDMUNDS
SUFFOLK • STATION 468

322 BG
449/450/451/452 BS

►Co-pilot Lt William Kinney, flight engineer and turret gunner S/Sgt John Muters and radio operator T/Sgt Bill Taylor pose with their assigned Marauder, about April 1943. *Gawja-Jerk* was never used on a combat mission as it lacked certain equipment deemed necessary for operations and was soon transferred from Bury St Edmunds to a training unit. The picture was taken by the pilot, Capt. Roland Scott, who was wounded on the first low-level mission undertaken with B-26s. Kinney flew co-pilot for Lt Col Bill Purinton, Group Executive, on the second, disastrous mission. He spent the rest of the war as a PoW after being shot down over the North Sea. (Roland Scott)

BURY ST EDMUNDS

94 BG
331/332/333/410 BS

▼ Maj. Byron E. Trent, last CO of the 333rd Bomb Squadron while at Bury, with a *Disney* 'rocket bomb'. The 94th Bomb Group received these missiles in the last month of hostilities for use in trials against enemy fortified concrete installations. The British-made weapon weighed 4,500lb and initially could only be carried externally on under-wing racks of B-17s: at 14 feet it was too long for stowing in the bays of British bombers. The rocket motor ignited at an altitude of approximately 5,000 feet and propelled the missile into its target at 2,400 feet per second. This is the second trial missile in the Bury St Edmunds bomb dump. The first trial against defences at Royan on 15 April 1945 was abortive when the missile failed to release properly and had to be jettisoned over the sea. It is believed that this second missile was never used in anger. (Byron E. Trent)

▼ *Ice Cold Katie* of the 332nd Bomb Squadron on an operation in April 1945. At this time the 94th Bomb Group had removed both chin and ball turrets in an experiment aimed at improving performance. The cheek, upper, waist and tail guns were retained.

Ice Cold Katie – the name derived from a popular song of the previous year – sports the red engine cowls and wing chevron that identified, respectively, the 322nd Bomb Squadron and the 94th Group within the 4th Combat Wing. (Byron E. Trent)

◀When chin turrets were removed from Fortresses of the 94th Group to improve performance, a few aircraft were provided with a single hand-held .50-calibre machine gun to fire through the nosepiece, in similar fashion to the installation in the old B-17Fs. One of these, 43-38825, is seen with the dark blue engine cowlings that identified the 331st Bomb Squadron. (Robert Astrella)

▲ After VE-Day the 94th Bomb Group was scheduled to remain in Europe as part of the occupational air forces. Most of its wartime aircraft were transferred to other groups and the 94th received many B-17s equipped with H2X radars from the home-going units. *The Mighty Mike* was one, a veteran of more than 30 missions with the 303rd Bomb Group at Molesworth. Here the aircraft is undergoing engine maintenance on hardstand No 17 looking north. (Byron E. Trent)

► One of the last new B-17Gs taken into service by the 8th Air Force, assigned to the 332nd Bomb Squadron, is seen here at Chalgrove in early May 1945. At this time the 94th was removing all chin and ball turrets from its aircraft. (Robert Astrella)

CHEDDINGTON
BUCKINGHAMSHIRE • STATION 113

NIGHT LEAFLET SQUADRON

◄ From the spring of 1944 the 8th Air Force utilized mobile instructional teams to keep the personnel of ground technical units up to date with the latest developments. Usually equipped with a large mobile workshop type trailer vehicle, each team specialized in particular aircraft types or major systems. The instruction on oxygen regulator changes to be found in new B-17 Fortresses depicted here was specially posed for an official photographer in front of a veteran B-17F aircraft of the unit. *Flak Alley Lil* flew twelve daylight bombing raids with the 305th Bomb Group in the summer of 1943 before the squadron to which she was assigned was detached to deliver propaganda leaflets over Germany and occupied Europe by night. Indicative of this work is the matt black paint on the aircraft's under surfaces. (USAAF K3020)

► B-17F *Cavalier* served with the 306th Bomb Group at Thurleigh from September 1943 to February 1944, when it was transferred to Cheddington. At this base it was used by the 8th Reconnaissance Courier Squadron, a provisional unit which had the combined duties of collecting and delivering photographic reconnaissance material at various bases and local and long-range weather flights. In May 1944 the unit was moved to Watton and was absorbed by the 8th Reconnaissance Weather Squadron (Heavy), which in August became regularized as the 652nd Bomb Squadron (R). Meteorological instruments can be seen fixed on each side of the Fortress's waist window. (Robert Astrella)

CHELVESTON

NORTHAMPTONSHIRE • STATION 105

305 BG
364/365/366/422 BS

▼ One of the most famous survival stories in VIII Bomber Command history is that of 1/Lt William D. Whitson's crew in B-17F *Old Bill* of the 305th Bomb Group. Repeatedly attacked by enemy fighters during an abortive mission on 15 May 1943, the Fortress received numerous hits from 20mm cannon shells and .30-calibre bullets that punctured the aircraft's skin in more than 500 places and wounded nine of the eleven men on board, one fatally. At this date the normal crew complement was ten, the additional man being a photographer. Co-pilot 2/Lt Harry L. Holt and top turret gunner Albert Hayman were seriously wounded by the 20mm shell that detonated on penetrating the side of the flight deck, leaving this large hole. (USAAF)

▼ The *Old Bill* motif was painted by Capt. Bruce Bairnsfather and based on the famous First World War cartoon character he created. (USAAF).

CHIPPING ONGAR

ESSEX • STATION 162

387 BG
556/557/558/559 BS

► Sgt James Stalnacker (left) and another member of the *Lucky Lady* ground crew smile for the camera. A B-26B inherited from another group, this aircraft was wrecked in a crash-landing on 25 May 1944. Having taken off for a combat mission, the aircraft experienced complete instrument failure and the pilot made an emergency landing on a cross runway, running off into some trees. (George Vasampaur)

▶ The crew of B-24H *Katrinka* don flying clothing after being trucked to their bomber. A pilot is fixing the yellow Mae West inflatable life jacket over his electrically heated flying suit. Chest parachute packs, steel 'flak' helmets and flying boots are to be seen among the equipment on the ground. The aircraft, named after a popular cartoon character, is about to leave on its eighth combat mission, late June 1944. (Mark Brown: Air Force Academy)

▶ *Leo*, a B-24H, was originally assigned to the 834th Bomb Squadron (known as the Zodiac Squadron) of the 486th Bomb Group at Sudbury. The painted-out identification marking for its first unit can be discerned on the rear fuselage. Transferred to the 493rd Bomb Group, the aircraft served with the 860th Bomb Squadron – as its yellow propeller bosses indicate. (Mark Brown: Air Force Academy)

▼ An 862nd Bomb Squadron B-24J starts down runway 16, late June 1944. (Mark Brown: Air Force Academy)

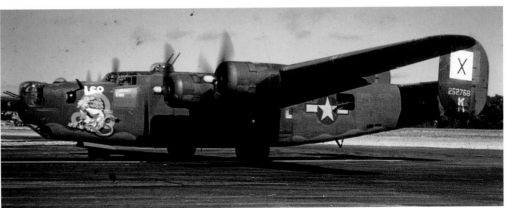

►One of the most distinguished pilots of the 4th Fighter Group, Don Gentile (centre), watching armourers working on the guns of his P-51B, about 1 April 1944. Much trouble was experienced with gun jams in this model Mustang owing to the canted positioning of the weapon in the wing. In the early days of service Mustang pilots sometimes returned from combat with only one gun operative. (USAAF K1908)

▼Col Donald J. M. Blakeslee, the dynamic and colourful commander of the 4th Fighter Group during its most successful period, seen with arm extended to close the canopy of his P-51D, August 1944. Don Blakeslee was a 'natural' fighter pilot and an excellent air leader. (USAAF K2438)

◄Crew chief Rod Lonier takes a break for a pipe on Lt Col Claiborne Kinnard's Mustang *Man o' War*. Kinnard commanded the 4th Fighter Group from August to late November 1944, having previously served with the 355th Fighter Group at Steeple Morden, from where the victories recorded on this Mustang were gained. He had no air victories while flying with the 4th. Note the twin rear mirrors on the windshield framing. (Edward Richie)

▲*Suzy*, a P-51D of the 336th Fighter Squadron, over East Anglia. The aircraft was shot down by ground fire during a strafing attack on an airfield near Munich on 9 April 1945. The pilot, Lt Robert Bucholz, was killed. (Mark Brown: Air Force Academy)

▲ While another Mustang cavorts in the sky, *Sunny VIII* lives up to its name on a bright spring day. This was Col Everett W. Stewart's aircraft, flown while commanding the 4th Fighter Group from February 1945 to the end of hostilities. Stewart, like Kinnard, had previously served with the 355th Fighter Group. The chief of the ground crew maintaining the Mustang was Sgt Glesner Weckbacker. (Glesner Weckbacker)

► An unknown ground crewman poses with *My Achin' Back*, a P-51D of the 334th Fighter Squadron, about April 1945. This eye-catching decoration was the work of Sgt Donald E. Allen, a crew chief, who was much in demand for his talent with a paint brush. (Larry Hendal)

▶ Sgt George Russell on the Mustang in his charge, in a photograph taken after the end of hostilities in the 334th Fighter Squadron dispersal area, looking north-east to beyond runway 17. *Jan* was the nickname of his previous Mustang; the art was more of Sgt Allen's handiwork. Although it was usually a pilot's prerogative to decide on a nickname or motif for the aircraft he was assigned, if inherited from another pilot the decor often remained unchanged. In some instances pilots simply had their own preference added, which often accounted for aircraft with two nicknames. In other cases the ground crew were permitted to select a name, and in still others it was a combination of pilot and ground crew choice. (Larry Hendel)

◀ On 23 March 1945, the day before the Allies launched their offensive across the Rhine, 8th Air Force fighter group commanders, or their representatives, flew to Debden for a meeting (similar get-togethers occurred periodically at selected bases). Shown here are 55th and 356th Fighter Group Mustangs and a Noorduyn UC-64 Norseman from the 479th Fighter Group. The P-51D of the 55th Group was usually flown by Lt Col John L. McGinn, Operations Officer of the Group, who had previously flown a tour on P-38s in the South-West Pacific area. The green used as the Group chequerboard marking is so dark as to almost appear black at a distance. These dull markings contrast with the scarlet nose superimposed with blue diamonds that distinguished the 356th Fighter Group. *Judy* was the assigned aircraft of Capt. Michael Yaunell. (Edward Richie)

▶ In the final months of the war most fighter groups had one or two two-seat conversions of the fighter type flown in order to aid the instruction of replacement pilots in special techniques and tactics employed by the unit. The Mustang supplied to the 4th for this purpose was a P-51B that had served with several organizations since November 1943, when it had been assigned to the first Mustang group to become operational in the UK. To effect seating for a passenger, the radio, battery and dynamotor were repositioned and the 85 US gallon fuel tank, to the rear of the cockpit, was completely removed with all its plumbing. In addition to the seat, an interphone for communication with the pilot, an oxygen supply and various duplicated cockpit instruments were installed. The position was very cramped in these conversions, which were performed mostly by base engineering. This aircraft has a red, white and blue divisioned rudder, indicating that it is assigned to the Group Operational Training Unit. (Edward Richie)

▲ The 65th Fighter Wing, controlling the 4th, 56th, 355th, 361st and 479th Groups and based in a commandeered school building in Saffron Walden, used the north-east corner of Debden for its staff aircraft. One of the most popular was a Piper L-4B (officially named Grasshopper but usually referred to by its civil aircraft type name, Cub), here being flown off the grass by Captain Jack Roberts in February 1945. Behind the 'shark mouth' painted on the nose are the alternating red and white stripes that identified most 65th Wing HQ aircraft. A thumbing cartoon character and *AH-OY*, painted near the entrance door, was more slogan than name. This view is to the north-east and the 334th Fighter Squadron's dispersal area. (Air Force Museum)

DEENETHORPE
NORTHAMPTONSHIRE • STATION 128

401 BG
612/613/614/615 BS

▶ A nameless pathfinder B-17G – with a radome in place of the ball turret – soon after it was received by the 615th Bomb Squadron in October 1944. This aircraft's operational life was short. On 11 December it was a stand-by spare and took off to catch the 401st Group formation when one of the pathfinder aircraft had mechanical difficulties. Unfortunately this replacement Fortress also suffered mechanical trouble and, with two engines out, Capt. Alva Chapman managed to bring it down safely at Brussels/Melsbroek airfield. While still under repair at this location it was destroyed by strafing German fighters on New Year's Day 1945. (Robert Astrella)

DEOPHAM GREEN
NORFOLK • STATION 142

▲ Accidents were a common feature of air operations during the Second World War and no unit of the 8th Air Force avoided these depressing incidents. Their frequency was due to a combination of factors, principally the inadequacy of aircraft and both air and ground crews in the environment in which they had to operate. The majority of men gave of their best but the technology of the time did not provide the safety factors that would secure flight in later years. Weather conditions often played a part in the demise of many aircraft. On 19 May 1944 the 45th Combat Wing was assembling formations over south Norfolk amid patches of cumulus. In the course of dodging round this, the 388th Bomb Group suddenly found itself on a collision course with the 452nd Bomb Group and as the formations tried to avoid each other one of the lower 388th Fortresses hit and severed the tail of a 452nd aircraft. Although damaged, the 388th B-17 crash-landed successfully at Watton; the 452nd machine, B-17G 42-38145, minus its tail, spun down to crash in a field at Folly Farm, New Buckenham. A photographer with a cine-camera, flying in a 93rd Bomb Group Liberator, took these photographs of the impact as a bomb and the fuel detonated. Two of the crew perished but eight were able to parachute safely. (Amos L. Golisch)

▼ A 729th Bomb Squadron B-17G, 43-38702, at a continental airfield for refuelling, about December 1944. (USAAF)

DUXFORD
CAMBRIDGESHIRE • STATION 357

▶ The black and white chequerboard cowls of the 78th Fighter Group provided probably the most striking identity markings of all 8th Air Force fighter organizations. This Thunderbolt of the 82nd Fighter Squadron, seen about July 1944, had, like many fighters, a brief operational life: it failed to return with Lt Richard D. Sharpe from a ground-strafing mission over the Low Countries on 3 September 1944. (USAF)

▶ An 83rd Fighter Squadron P-51D, 44-63271, flying over Duxford about early February 1945. (C. Tom Bendorf)

▼ A long shot of 83rd Fighter Squadron P-51 Mustang 'HL:F' coming in to land with drop tanks still under its wings. The photograph was taken from the south-east side of the airfield, looking north-west across the head of the runway towards the 84th Fighter Squadron blister hangars and dispersal area. Beyond is the A505 main road. At the time Duxford had a single steel mat runway over turf. (C. Tom Bendorf)

▶ 'There is many a boy here who looks on war as all glory but, boys, it is all hell.' These famous words of Civil War General Sherman inspired the slogan *Sherman Was Right!* on 1/Lt Frank E. Oiler's Mustang. It was prophetically true, as this 84th Fighter Squadron aircraft was lost on an escort mission on 3 March 1945 with Lt Loius R. Hereford. (C. Tom Bendorf)

◄ Lt Col John Landers, Group CO, with cumbersome parachute and dinghy attached, is assisted into the cockpit of *Anne Nihilator* prior to a mission, about March 1945. The aircraft was previously the 'mount' of Lt Col Gilbert. In the second picture the crew chief has cleared the aircraft and in the third the engine is running and the aircraft ready to move. Note the map resting against the inner windshield, where it can be easily reached for consulting. The location is the first blast-protected aircraft standings to the west of the hangars. (Mason Barnard Jr).

► 1/Lt Earl Stier managed to fly this Mustang, 'WZ:Y', back to home base on 1 March 1945 after a direct hit from shell flak had blasted away a considerable area of the fin and rudder. The black rudder identified the 84th Fighter Squadron. (C. Tom Bendorf)

◄ On a wet winter's day, Brig. Gen. Woodbury, who commanded the 66th Fighter Wing to which the 78th Fighter Group was assigned, talks to senior officers. The general's staff car carries the star on red backing that identifies the rank of the occupant. The photograph was taken at the Duxford parade ground on the occasion of an award presentation. (Mason Barnard Jr)

▼ The main entrance to Duxford airfield, looking north-west, spring 1945. Officers and enlisted men are walking from the living site areas across the A505 Royston–Newmarket public road. The Officers' Mess building can be seen on the extreme right, on the far side of the road. The sentry hut notice warns that military vehicles are not to leave the technical site unless on official business. This spot is now the main entrance to the Imperial War Museum at Duxford. (Mason Barnard Jr)

◀ Big green noses identified 359th Fighter Group Mustangs. This example is 415717 'CV:Q', the usual 'mount' of Maj. Niven Cranfill, who flew 133 combat hours in eight months and had five air victories while operating from East Wretham. His Mustang was photographed at Debden when, as Group Operations Officer, he was attending a briefing of fighter group leaders prior to the airborne assault across the Rhine on 24 March 1945. (Ed Richie)

ELVEDEN HALL
SUFFOLK • STATION 116

HQ 3 AD

▼ The country seat of Lord Iveagh, a member of the prosperous Guinness brewing famiiy, was taken over by the Air Ministry and in 1942 allocated to the USAAF. The first operational occupants were personnel of HQ 3rd Bomb Wing controlling fifteen airfields built, building and projected, of which three were situated in south-west Norfolk and the rest in central and west Suffolk. Only Rougham (Bury St Edmunds), Honington, Horham, Snetterton Heath and Rattlesden received air units before the 3rd Bomb Wing exchanged areas and headquarters with the 4th Bomb Wing at Marks Hall, Essex. The 3rd Wing's combat groups flew medium bombers, the 4th's heavy, so the transfer placed the mediums, with their more limited endurance, closer to potential targets in occupied Europe. The 4th Bomb Wing officially took up residence at Elveden Hall in June 1943, its designation being changed to 3rd Bomb Division that September to embrace its expanding strength and again, on 1 January 1945, to 3rd Air Division to signify its control of both bomber and fighter units. It was then, in effect, an air force within an air force. The photograph shows the entrance to the main building with the Stars and Stripes on the flagpole, about July 1944. (Mark Brown: Air Force Academy)

▲ *The Jinx* had an array of bad luck symbols decorating the side of its nose. If this was intended to help ward off misfortune it appears to have been successful as the aircraft survived an operational career to be broken up in the UK as no longer fit for flying in May 1945. It was named by Lt Thomas Keyes' crew, who were crew No 13 of the 490th's original air echelon. The crew chief of this B-24H was Sgt John S. Hancock. The white band along the edge of the bomb bay doors provided a visual indicator to the crews of other Liberators in a formation as to what extent the electrically operated doors were open, much trouble having been experienced with the doors 'edging' from the desired position. The picture was taken in June 1944 on hardstanding No 37 looking due north; No 2 hangar is seen far left. The bombs left by the hardstand made excellent cycle props. (Mark Brown: Air Force Academy)

▼ A photograph taken in the winter of 1944–45: two B-17s, back from a mission, are on the runway with about a half a mile's separation and a third is on its approach. (Mark Brown: Air Force Academy)

▲ An aerial view of Station 134, from directly over the village of Yaxley and looking along the line of the A140 public road towards Scole on the Suffolk/Norfolk county boundary, spring 1945. The designers of the airfield took the unusual step of placing a group of hardstandings on the west side of the A140. This necessitated the closing of this main Ipswich–Norwich road every time aircraft moved to and from this dispersal area. Gates were put across the road near each crossing point and guards were always on duty. Even though wartime road traffic was limited, this arrangement proved a great inconvenience both to the airfield administration and to the general public. With the exception of that facing the butts, all aircraft hardstandings at Eye were of the loop type. Although a loop was designed to take a single heavy bomber, it was common practice at all 8th Air Force bases to park two on each loop, as can be seen here. This was a result of the fact that the average complement of a heavy bomb group was in excess of the 50 hardstandings provided, the aircraft complement having expanded from 32 in 1942 to 72 in 1945. (Mark Brown: Air Force Academy)

▶ A '6 × 6' truck collects fliers from a recently returned B-17G on hardstand 41 in the 848th Bomb Squadron aircraft dispersal area, looking north-east along the perimeter track near the start of runway 09. (Mark Brown: Air Force Academy)

► High-explosive bombs in a revetment serving the 851st Bomb Squadron, with a small caterpillar-tracked loading crane in the foreground and two tricycle bomb-carrying trollies park on the parallel roadway. Unlike many airfield bomb dumps in East Anglia, that at Eye did not have the benefit of being located in a wooded area to serve both as camouflage and a means of lessening blast in the case of an accidental detonation, although the low soil mounds on each side of the bomb store pads were designed to give some blast protection. The photograph was taken from the revetments nearest hardstands 27 and 28 on the south-east side of the airfield, looking towards the north-west. (Mark Brown: Air Force Academy)

▲ An 851st Bomb Squadron Fortress returns from a mission and is about to touch down on runway 27. The photograph was taken looking north-east towards houses on the Brome–Eye road. (Arnold N. Delmonico)

◄ The 490th BG command evidently took a liberal view of the sexually suggestive artwork that appeared on its aircraft. Particularly famous was *Bobby Sox*, where the artist made good use of the young lady's rear anatomy. This B-17G was transferred to the 94th Bomb Group in May 1945. (Mark Brown: Air Force Academy)

▶ Another equally daring nickname was *£5 with Breakfast*, reflecting the usual terms of better-class London prostitutes of the day. (Arnold N. Delmonico)

▼ *Carolina Moon* piled up 78 combat missions, more than any other 490th B-17. It was common practice to paint on the names of wives and girlfriends near flight stations – these looked good in photographs sent home! (Arnold N. Delmonico)

▶ More eye-catching artwork in the 851st Bomb Squadron was that on *Looky Looky*. The figure was originally intended to be completely nude, but there was finally some acknowledgement of modesty. (Arnold N. Delmonico)

▼ The gorgeous girl on *Alice Blue Gown* was well known at Eye. This 851st Bomb Squadron B-17G completed 67 missions. (Arnold N. Delmonico)

▶ Under full power, *Love 'Em All* thunders down runway 21. By the end of hostilities this 849th Bomb Squadron Fortress would carry 40 bomb symbols for combat missions, two swastikas for enemy fighter claims and six parcels for food drops over Holland. (Arnold N. Delmonico)

▼ In the morning of 6 February 1945, *Big Poison* was climbing through murk during assembly when, at approximately 6,000 feet, its left wing struck that of a 388th Bomb Group Fortress. Both crews baled out but one man's parachute failed to open. The wreck of *Big Poison* fell on cottages at Prickwillow, Cambridgeshire, killing two civilians. (Arnold N. Delmonico)

▶ *Swede*, a worn P-51B of the 504th Fighter Squadron, late October 1944. Few of this model remained in combat units by this date, the average life of a fighter aircraft being but a few weeks. The name resulted from the pilot's Swedish forebears, Lt Duane Larson being assigned this aircraft. (Robert Astrella)

▼ Pilots were acutely aware of how much their safety depended on the quality of work performed by the ground crew and liked to show these men how much they were appreciated. One way was to have

the ground crew included when pictures were taken of the pilot and his aircraft. Here Capt. L. Jeffery French sits on the wing of *Rusty* beside S/Sgt Robert Burns, the crew chief. When French finished his tour in January 1945, *Rusty* was taken over by 2/Lt William R. Preddy, brother of the top scoring Mustang ace Maj. George Preddy who, tragically, had been killed the previous month by fire from US ground forces. Bill Preddy was flying *Rusty* when he was shot down and killed near Prague on 17 April 1945. (James R. Starnes)

▼ One of the most successful ground strafers at Fowlmere was Maj. Archie Tower, the last wartime CO of the 505th Fighter Squadron. His *Lucky Boy* displays twenty victory symbols for eighteen ground 'kills' and two air, one of which latter was shared with another pilot. Propeller specialist Sgt Carl Hicks, crew chief Ted Sulima and his assistant Herbert Ward pose for the camera. (James R. Starnes)

▼ The aircraft dispersal area of the 504th Fighter Squadron, which had its Mustangs' rudders painted a medium green. The standings were chiefly secured wooden plank panels bordering the concrete perimeter track. This photograph, dated about summer 1945, was taken looking west from a point beside the perimeter track opposite the easternmost blister hangar. (James R. Starnes)

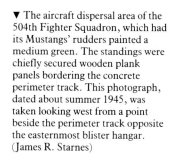

▶ One of four aircraft named *Tar Heel* (indicative of the pilot's home state, North Carolina) flown by Capt. James R. Starnes. On 4 August 1944, when a first lieutenant, Jim Starnes shot down an enemy fighter to become the third member of the 339th to reach 'ace' status (i.e., with five or more enemy aircraft destroyed in combat). His total victories at VE-Day were six air and six ground. *Tar Heel* has a K-25 camera mounted on the back of the seat armour plate panel protecting the pilot from the rear. The purpose of the camera was to take oblique photographs of strafed targets or anything observed in enemy territory that might interest military intelligence. The four enlisted men posing by the Mustang when this picture was taken in June 1945 are, left to right, S/Sgt Leslie Harbold, Sgt Carl Hicks, T/Sgt Joe Par and S/Sgt Fred Nessler. They were not Starnes' ground crew. (James R. Starnes)

► Lt Col William C. Clark in his P-51D *Happy IV*. The name *Dotty*, part of which can be seen on the canopy frame, was that of his wife. Bill Clark, who took command of the 339th in the last month of hostilities, had previously been the Group Air Executive and CO of the 504th Fighter Squadron. Nazi flags signify nine enemy aircraft credited destroyed – one in the air and eight on the ground. At this time the 8th Air Force rated air and ground victories of equal status because of the danger involved in strafing enemy airfields. Crew chief S/Sgt Bennie Kennedy stands on the other side of the cockpit. (James R. Starnes)

▼ *Mariam* sits at Eye while B-17s return from a mission. The pilot of the Mustang, Capt. Harry Corey, had 'dropped in' to visit a friend. (Arnold N. Delmonico)

► A B-17G of the 571st Bomb Squadron flying over flooded farmland in the Netherlands on 6 May 1945. The aircraft was on approach to the marked area at Utrecht to drop food containers for the starving Dutch populace. (Mark Brown: Air Force Academy)

◄ An unnamed Fortress, 43-38837 'CC:D', of the 569th Bomb Squadron, on pan hardstand No 18 about May 1945. The blue nose band was a squadron identity marking. This picture was taken looking in a south-westerly direction. (Unknown USAAF)

► Lt Col Robert W. Waltz, 390th Bomb Group Operations Officer (seated), and Maj. Russell F. Brannen, Assistant Operations Officer, at work on a mission schedule. Bob Waltz, an original member of the Group, remained with it throughout hostilities, flying 42 combat missions. He was also one of the most highly decorated members of the 390th. Russ Brannen flew his first mission on D-Day and had 43 to his credit by VE-Day. The wall board on the right is the aircraft status chart, the chalked numbers being the 'last three' of the aircraft's serial numbers. The board behind the desk, above the loudspeaker, carries the names of crew captains and the number of missions each has flown. (390th Bomb Group Association)

► 'Bluebell D-Dog' identified this Fortress over the air waves. Bluebell was the radio call-sign of the 750th Bomb Squadron during the last year of hostilities. Visually, the Squadron's aircraft could be recognized by their white-painted propeller bosses. (Leslie R. Peterson)

▼ Connington church tower shines in the late afternoon winter sunshine, viewed from a returning Fortress circling for its landing approach. Glatton airfield was built between the villages of Connington and Holme, whereas the parish of Glatton is to the west of the A1 Great North Road – the line of which is at the top left-hand corner of the photograph. B-17s can be seen in the dispersal area behind the church and the Nissen huts of several accommodation sites are visible close to the village. (Leslie R. Peterson)

▶Contrails flow from 457th Bomb Group Fortresses heading for the target at five miles plus above the Earth. The temperature at this altitude ranged from 30 to 50° below freezing. (Leslie R. Peterson)

◀*Rene V* of the 750th Bomb Squadron was the personal B-17 of the 457th Bomb Group's original combat commander, Col James Luper, and was named after his wife. Luper's first combat B-17, which happened to be the one-thousandth Fortress produced by the Douglas factory, was named *Rene III* and by the summer of 1944 had been retired as the CO's steed in favour of a new B-17G which became *Rene IV*. Number four did not endure for long and *Rene V*, another silver B-17G, was secured. Luper, a West Point officer very popular with his men, was shot down leading a mission to the Politz oil installations on 7 October 1944 and taken prisoner. He was not flying in *Rene V*, which continued in combat missions until the end of hostilities. *Rene III* also continued to serve, only to be lost in March 1945 on its 105th mission. (Leslie R. Peterson)

▼ One-thousand-pound high-explosive bombs dropping in train from 457th BG B-17s on 10 April 1945. Although this was a visual sighting drop, Sky Markers were still released. The chemical mixture that made the white smoke often had a caustic effect on aircraft Plexiglas. Soon after these photographs were taken the 457th formation was attacked by Me 262 jet fighters and two of the B-17s failed to return. (Arthur Fitch)

▲ A veteran 750th Bomb Squadron B-17G landing at Mount Farm, summer 1944. (Robert Astrella)

GRAFTON UNDERWOOD
NORTHAMPTONSHIRE • **STATION 106**

384 BG
544/545/546/547 BS

▶ The 384th Bomb Group over a target at Koblenz on 24 December 1944. The B-17G Fortress on the right, 42-97960, was lost to flak over Berlin on 3 February 1945. (Leslie R. Peterson)

▲ Shimmering in morning sunlight, a Fortress goes to war. The letter 'G' on a square insignia of the 385th was painted out or removed when the Group was transferred from the 4th to the 93rd Wing in 1945. Photographed in the autumn of 1944, this B-17G survived the war, having flown 119 missions with only one turnback for mechanical reasons. (Clark B. Rollins)

▼ Squadron COs anxiously check in bombers landing from a mission. Note the chequered Flying Control trailer, from which close proximity runway control was handled by the duty operator with flare signal pistol and Aldis lamp. The weather-protective transparency on top of the trailer is a B-17F nosepiece. This picture was taken when the trailer was situated to the right of the head of runway 25. (Clark B. Rollins)

▶ Left waist gunner and Assistant Flight Engineer, S/Sgt Alva Woodall, at his station in a B-17F of the 551st Bomb Squadron. The various inscriptions are his suggestions for a name for the bomber assigned to 1/Lt Forrest Poore's crew. Part of the flexible ammunition trace feed can be seen looped at the right of the window. Woodall was killed when the crew were shot down in another B-17F on 11 December 1943. (Linn C. Stuckenbruck)

◀ Capt. Mark Brown, 3rd Division HQ Photographic Officer, in flight clothing prior to boarding *Ole Doodle Bug* for a food-dropping mission to Utrecht on May Day 1945. The red chequerboard group identification marking, introduced when the 385th was transferred to the 93rd Combat Wing, was somewhat demanding of the painter's time and took several weeks to effect on all aircraft. Mark Brown – who is responsible for many of the colour photographs reproduced in this volume – wears A-11 coverall trousers and a B-15 collared jacket. He has a harness with steel rings to take the chest-type parachute he is holding (one of the securing snap rings faces the camera). The helmet appears to be an RAF C-type. (Mark Brown: Air Force Academy)

▲ Co-pilot Lt Clark Rollins Jr takes a look out of the pilot's window. *Madam Shoo Shoo*, often a 'lead ship' of the 551st Bomb Squadron, had its insignia painted by Ann Hayward. A 'flak patch' covered a splinter hole in the word 'Madam'. The shell fragment, entering here, tore up navigator John Gotwald's desk without injuring him. (Clark B. Rollins)

▼ As part of a publicity project, the US Forces daily newspaper, *Stars and Stripes*, organized a competition to find 'the most beautiful WAC' serving in England. The resultant vote awarded the distinction to Pfc Ruby Newell from Long Beach, California. To mark the event a bomber was to be named in her honour and an aircraft of the 549th Bomb Squadron was selected. Cpl William Ploss, a talented artist serving at Great Ashfield, was commissioned to paint a likeness of Miss Newell on the B-17 and a christening ceremony was arranged. A pair of steps allowed the pretty WAC to pose against *Ruby's Raiders* for photographers. The Fortress was lost on 24th March 1945. (Clark B. Rollins)

► Ann Hayward was a young English girl whose artistic talents were employed to paint unofficial insignia on aircraft at the request of 385th personnel. As a reward, it was suggested she name a Fortress for herself and the result was *Haybag Annie*. This 550th Bomb Squadron B-17G had completed 105 missions by VE-Day but was damaged beyond repair in an accident. (Mark Brown: Air Force Academy)

▶ As the 385th heads for home, a combat wing of bombers heads for the target, its passage through the sub-stratosphere plainly visible. (Clark B. Rollins)

▼ With landing gear and bomb doors open to reduce air speed, 385th B-17s prepare to unload food containers at Utrecht during May 1945. The aircraft with the chequerboard tail is the fairly new B-17G 43-39117 'K'. The camouflaged aircraft is *Jerry Boy*, a veteran that had recently suffered tail damage. (Mark Brown: Air Force Academy)

▲ Farm workers carting oat straw at Bacon Farm, Stebbing, beside the last hardstanding on the south side of the western end of the main runway: a view looking east of north past the butts on the far side of the airfield, around 1 September 1943. The Marauder beside the fuel bowser, *Bag of Bolts* of the 450th Bomb Squadron, went missing on the night of 7/8 July 1944, flying its 98th mission. (USAF K1147)

▼ B-26B *Bag of Bolts* viewed from another 450th Bomb Squadron aircraft while flying close formation over Essex. (Roland Scott)

▶ *El Diablo*, with nine missions to its credit, survived to fly back to the US in May 1944. (USAAF)

▼ Three captains: left to right, Louis Sebille, Roland Scott and Howard Posson, who all took part in the first Marauder combat mission flown from England. Scott lost an eye on that occasion and was here visiting his friends at Andrews Field before returning to the US. Louis Sebille was killed flying a Mustang during the Korean War in an action that earned a Medal of Honor. (Roland Scott)

▲ A posed view of Capt. Walker ('Bud') Mahurin on his P-47 talking to its crew chief, S/Sgt John E. Barnes. The aircraft had been 'bought' by the citizens of Atlantic City, New Jersey – that is, they had purchased government war bonds to the value of the cost of a fighter, approximately $105,000. This was acknowledged with a suitable painting of Atlantic City's choice, which was applied before the aircraft was shipped overseas from the factory. The 56th Fighter Group was a recipient of several of these presentation aircraft. Mahurin was the first 8th Air Force fighter pilot to take his score of victories into double figures. His eventual tally was 21 in the air before being shot down by the gunner of a Dornier bomber he was attacking over France. Evading capture, he later flew against the Japanese to add another victory. In the Korean War Mahurin was credited with three MiGs and shared in the destruction of another before being shot down himself and made prisoner. (USAAF Official)

▼ Lucky Little Devil was the name of the P-47C flown by 1/Lt John W. Vogt Jr in the 63rd Fighter Squadron. One of the first Thunderbolts received by the 56th after arrival in England – on 8 February 1943 – it was transferred to the 365th Fighter Group, a 9th Air Force organization, at Gosfield, on 26 January 1944. Johnny Vogt shot down three enemy aircraft with this Thunderbolt and two more flying with the 56th before going to the 356th Fighter Group at Martlesham to raise the unit's combat experience level. Fighter pilots usually tried to have the initial letter of their surname as the individual plane-in-squadron letter of their aircraft, as was the case with Vogt. The photographer's shadow is of crew chief Frank Gyidik.

▲ A view across the perimeter track towards hardstand 45, January 1944. Originally known as 'belly tanks' because of their attachment to the shackles on the underside of a P-47's fuselage and later, more commonly, as 'drop tanks', the auxiliary fuel tanks visible here were essential to providing the thirsty Thunderbolt with sufficient range for bomber escort. The light grey painted pile in the foreground are 105 US gallon capacity, sheet steel type. The silver finished tanks of the same capacity in the background were made of a paper and plastic composition. Both came from British production sources.

The further P-47D, 27853, was the personal aircraft of the 63rd Fighter Squadron's CO, Maj. Sylvester Burke. (Air Force Museum)

▲ A 63rd Fighter Squadron P-47D Thunderbolt crosses the threshold of runway 29 as it returns from a mission in January 1943. The Fordson WOT 1 crash truck and GMC ambulance are parked on one of the roads leading to the bomb dump. This is a view looking north-east towards the butts. (Air Force Museum)

▶ *Princess Pat* was the assigned aircraft of 1/Lt Charles Reed, who joined the 63rd Fighter Squadron in August 1943 and was credited with 2¼ enemy aircraft destroyed in combat during his tour (the fraction is through sharing a credit with other pilots). (Alexander C. Sloan)

◀ The first 56th Fighter Group pilot to become an ace was Capt. Gerald W. Johnson, who achieved this unofficial status on 19 August 1943, the photograph being taken soon after the event. Gerry Johnson, also the second fighter ace in the 8th Air Force, rose in a long service career to the rank of lieutenant general and command of the Force. *In the Mood*, reflecting the famous Glenn Miller melody, was a presentation aircraft for Jackson County, Michigan. The white nose and wing bands were type recognition markings to help Allied pilots identify the Thunderbolt as friendly. These were thought necessary at the time of its operational début as the only other radial engined fighter in the theatre was the enemy Fw 190. The ground crew 'got busy' for this photograph. The 75 US gallon disposable fuel tank under the belly was just being introduced at this time, enabling the P-47 groups to extend their range. (USAAF Official)

◀ Lt Adam 'Wiskey' Wisniewski and Capt. Walker Mahurin indicating the point of action after a mission in January 1944. The Intelligence Officer is David W. Robinson, known affectionately to all as 'The Silver Fox'. Mahurin was the leading ace fighter pilot in the 8th Air Force at this time. (Air Force Museum)

◀ A January 1944 briefing. The CO of the 63rd Fighter Squadron, Maj. Sy Burke, sits in the front row with Lts Mike Quirk and Cal Reeder of the 62nd Squadron. Quirk was credited with twelve air and five ground victories during his tour. Immediately behind Burke is John Patton of the 63rd, who was shot down by an Fw 190 on 5 February 1944. In the fourth row are several 61st Fighter Squadron aces: from the aisle, Don Smith (6 victories), Joe Powers (14½), Bob Johnson (27) and, at the end, Jim Carter (6). Sitting behind Powers is Frank Klibbe (7 victories). (Air Force Museum)

► B-24 Liberator bombers replaced the P-47 Thunderbolts at Halesworth in April 1944. The 489th Bomb Group's identification marking was a bright green vertical tail surface with a white vertical stripe thereon. Sporting this decoration in the 846th Bomb Squadron dispersal area is *Callipygia*, a B-24H model. Beyond, another B-24 makes a low approach to the airfield. The British bus, painted in US Army Olive Drab, was a vehicle provided for use by the American Red Cross as a Clubmobile. Staffed by two girls, it visited all parts of the base each day, dispensing coffee and doughnuts. *Callipygia* was transferred to the 446th Bomb Group at Bungay when the 489th was withdrawn from combat and was destroyed in a non-combat crash on 1 February 1945. (Wallace A. Portouw)

► Smoke streams back from the No 2 engine of *The Ripper* on hardstanding 26 as it comes to life. Two members of the aircraft's ground crew stand in a position to signal the pilot in this photograph taken to south of west from hardstanding No 27. (Wallace A. Portouw)

▼ In August 1944 the 489th Bomb Group was transferred from the

disbanded 95th Combat Wing to the 20th Combat Wing and in consequence the tail colours were changed from green and white to an all-over yellow. Wearing the new livery, B-24H 42-94860 '8R:X' is seen reposing on hardstanding No 26, viewed from the perimeter track looking north. (Robert H. Buck)

▲ The 846th's Bomb Squadron's *Apassionato*, a 'silver' B-24H, viewed on hardstand number 24 – the next west from 26 – in October 1944. (Robert H. Buck)

▼ *Lil' Cookie* has a wheel change. This yellow polka dot 'assembly ship', used as a marker aircraft for assembling formations, was inherited from the 44th Bomb Group at Shipdham where it had seen several months of conventional combat operation. The 489th Bomb Group wing marking, 'W' in a circle, can be seen in this view from hardstanding No 2 looking north-west. (Wallace A. Portouw)

◄Another view of the 'assembly ship', showing the five signal lamps in the modified tail-end compartment. These flashed a cross-shaped signal. Other signal lamps were fixed in the fuselage sides for use in identifying the 489th formation in darkness or poor visibility. A low-flying B-24 can be seen in the distance. (Wallace A. Portouw)

HALESWORTH

5 ERS

► Soon after the Air Sea Rescue Squadron moved from Boxted to Halesworth and was designated the 5th Emergency Rescue Squadron, six OA-10 Catalina amphibians were assigned to the unit. Canadian-built by Vickers, they were painted white overall but carried no unit markings. Individual names and motifs were painted on several of these aircraft. This is *Sophisticat* with its ground crew working on engines – S/Sgt G. E. Parks, crew chief, on the left engine and his assistant, Pfc U. V. Weinberg, on the right. (USAAF K3641)

▶ *Jerk's Natural* was named after John Jerstad, the 328th Bomb Squadron pilot who flew this B-24D to the UK among the initial complement of the 93rd Bomb Group. The record of the crew and bomber is displayed on the nose: the submarine is for a U-boat claimed sunk in the Gulf of Mexico before flying overseas; the five crosses represent enemy fighters claimed destroyed by its gunners; the first nine yellow bomb symbols are for bombing raids carried out in 1942 from Alconbury; the two black bombs and fourteen red bombs are for raids carried out from North African bases in darkness and daylight; and the last

five yellow bombs are for missions flown from Hardwick in the spring and summer of 1943 before the aircraft went to North Africa again to take part in the famous low-level raid on the Ploesti oil fields in Romania. After flying *Jerk's Natural* on five early missions from England, John Jerstad received promotion and the aircraft was taken over by another pilot. Jerstad was killed at Ploesti, earning his country's highest award for bravery; his old bomber, flown by another pilot, survived, only to be lost on a mission flown to Austria on 1 October 1943. (USAAF Official)

◀ Four famous B-24Ds of the 93rd in flight over England, about July 1943. All took part in, and survived, the low-level raid on the Romanian oil refineries on 1 August 1943. *Joisey Bounce* had its named changed to *Utah Man* when taken over by Capt. Walt Stewart, after his home state. The aircraft was eventually lost with another crew on the Bremen mission of 13 November 1943. Partly hidden by *Joisey Bounce* is *The Duchess*, which completed 54 missions without a turnback for mechnical reasons, only to go missing in action with Lt David Thompson's crew on 25 February 1944. Both these aircraft were assigned to the 330th Bomb Squadron at the time of the photograph, identified by the radio-call letters' being positioned under the aircraft number on the tail and having a horizontal bar painted below. The two higher aircraft were assigned to the 328th Bomb Squadron (letters above the tail number), the nearest being *Bomerang*, which became the first 8th Air Force Liberator flying from England to complete 50 missions. The aircraft was retired and sent back to the USA in April 1944. The furthest B-24 is *Thundermug*, then a comparatively new arrival at Hardwick, which was written off as salvage in October 1943. Note that *Bomerang* has an RAF-type red, white and blue tail flash, a marking applied to those Liberators sent to support the North African campaign in December 1942. (USAAF K2073)

▶ The first special 'assembly' or 'formation' aircraft to appear with bright colours was *Ball of Fire*, an original B-24D brought to the UK by the 93rd Bomb Group and retired from combat duties in the autumn of 1943. The original 'barber's pole' paintwork on this aircraft was an intended red, white and blue, although the blue was actually a pale blue-grey. (Amos L. Golisch)

◄ During the German Ardennes offensive of the winter of 1944–45, bomber crews were often required to take off in appalling weather, with none of the aids to bad-weather flying that gave safety in later years: in the Second World War it was, as said, 'seat of your pants piloting'. In the freezing fog of the morning of 19 December 1944 the 93rd Bomb Group launched a mission in visiblity of less than 500 feet. The first B-24, hitting tree-tops beyond the end of the main runway, crashed in a potato field at Burnt Oak Farm, Aldeburgh, and burned out. What little remained of the wreckage, photographed about an hour later, shows the extent of the fog. The crew of eleven were all killed. (Glenn Tessmer)

► To delay the Allied advance into Holland, many low-lying areas near the Scheldt estuary were flooded by the Germans; the posts had been erected at an earlier date to prevent an airborne landing with gliders. The area had been liberated when this picture was taken from a low-flying B-24 returning from a mission. (Glenn Tessmer)

► From the co-pilot's seat of a Liberator going to war and heading out over the North Sea for Holland, Lt Glenn Tessmer snapped this unusual picture of a V-2 rocket trailing into the sub-stratosphere. (Glenn Tessmer)

◄ A view from the co-pilot's window of a 329th Bomb Squadron pathfinder B-24 equipped with G-H and distinguished by a red nose, approaching its target on 24 December 1944. The spent Sky Marker plumes of preceding formations are seen in the distance. (Glenn Tessmer)

HESTON

MIDDLESEX • **STATION 510**

27 TG

▼ A C-47 Skytrain wearing the double yellow bar tail-flash that marked aircraft of Air Service Command, about summer 1944. The insignia of the nose is that of one of the squadrons of the 27th Transport Group which plied between AFSC establishments in the UK or those in liberated France. Behind the C-47 is the 3rd Bomb Division HQ's *Silver Queen*, the first B-17 to be denuded of paint (in the summer of 1943) and used as a personal transport by General LeMay and his successor. (Mark Brown: Air Force Academy)

▲ The 389th's first assembly ship was known as *The Green Dragon*, a name derived from the Group's insignia, in turn adopted from a local pub sign (although the actual device used a colour more blue than green!). This old war-weary B-24D, originally with the 93rd Bomb Group at Hardwick, was wrecked after crash-landing at Manston as a result of landing gear problems on 25 July 1944. (John Driscoll)

◀ A B-24H on approach to Hethel, about April 1944. (USAAF K3913)

▼ Armament Officer Capt. John Driscoll beside the 566th Bomb Squadron veteran *Fightin' Sam* parked on hardstand 37. The insignia is based on the Li'l Abner strip cartoon character and was adopted as the Squadron's unofficial insignia. This B-24D was subsequently transferred to the 801st Bomb Group for supplying clandestine organizations in occupied Europe and later to similar work over the Balkans operating from Italy. (John Driscoll)

►*Southern Queen II* of the 566th Bomb Squadron coming in to land on runway 06, about April 1944. (USAAF).

▼*Delectable Doris*, with its striking nude, was named after the English girlfriend (later wife) of the crew chief; she was later at pains to stress that she did not pose for the likeness and that it was all the result of the artist's imagination! The B-24J was one of two lost during raids on targets at Magdeburg on 3 February 1945. In the early 1970s entrepreneur David Tallichet purchased a B-24L from India which spent some months at Duxford, the Imperial War Museum's airfield, en route to America. While there it was painted to represent *Delectable Doris* with an excellent reproduction of the original nose art by artist Gerry Collins. The bogus *Delectable Doris*, one of the few Liberators still flying, became a much photographed attraction at US airshows over the next two decades. This reproduction is of the real *Doris*, about autumn 1944. (Lucius R. Ades)

▲ Outright vulgar or obscene names were not allowed and 8th Air Force HQ, with an eye to censorship, asked units to submit a regular listing of what appeared on their aircraft. As policing proved so difficult the requirement was not adhered to and individual group headquarters were held responsible for effecting some control. However, if they could get away with it, cocking a snook at authority gave some pleasure to young airmen and thus a double meaning in aircraft names was not uncommon. *The Bigast Boid* was comparatively mild but a good enough laugh for flight engineer Leon Nowicki to select the background when having his picture taken. Note the nose skin bulging due to over-stressing. (Lucius R. Ades)

► At dusk on the evening of *22 April 1944* the *Luftwaffe* made one of its rare attempts to wreak havoc among returning US bombers as they prepared to land at their bases. They had undeniable success, as fourteen heavy bombers were shot down or wrecked in crashes and others badly damaged. A B-24J, shot-up in the darkness while coming in to land at Hethel, crashed into the radar building, killing two occupants, but the bomber's crew all escaped. The morning after, the scene in front of hangar line was one of devastation, with the remains of an outer wall of the building in the foreground of this photograph. The aircraft, one of the first models with silver finish, was burned out. One of the spectators is a Red Cross girl. It will be seen that the Hethel hangars bore 'shadow shaded' camouflage of irregular areas of green, light brown and black paint. Usually, only the hangars on those airfields completed in 1942 were so painted:

most T2 hangars erected in 1943 and 1944 were painted matt black. (John Driscoll)

▼ The occasion of the presentation of the Distinguished Unit Citation to the 389th Bomb Group, 9 May 1944. The saluting podium was positioned on the side of runway 17-35, in front of the hangars. Awaiting the presentation of colours are, left to right, Gen. Carl Spaatz, Commander US Strategic Air Forces in Europe; Col Robert B. Miller, CO 389th BG; Lt Gen. James H. Doolittle, Commander 8th Air Force; Maj. Gen. James P. Hodges, Commander 2nd Bomb Division; and Brig. Gen. Edward Timberlake Jr, CO 2nd Bomb Wing (of which the 389th was a component). The veteran B-24D drawn up behind the podium and weighed down with spectators is *Old Irish*. (Robert B. Miller)

◄ The Catholic chaplain at Hethel was Father Gerald Beck, who was particularly popular as he had flown on a few combat missions – without official permission. Very much a soldier's priest who regularly intermingled with personnel at both work and play, he was known as 'White Flak'. The nickname derived from his white hair – he was born in 1900 – and he had a sharp tongue should he disapprove of any man's conduct. He is pictured here preparing to take Communion in the hut used as the base chapel. (USAAF)

▲ Daws Hill Lodge, formerly part of Wycombe Abbey Girls' School and once the seat of the Marquis of Lincolnshire, was used as quarters and offices for the personnel of 8th Air Force Headquarters. A much-told anecdote was of the officer who, upon taking up residence when the building was first occupied by VIII Bomber Command, found a push-button on the wall behind his bed with a small sign reading 'Ring for Mistress'. This photograph was taken in the late summer of 1944, looking north-west towards the town. (John R. Johnson)

◄ Maj. Gen. Ira Eaker, commander of the 8th Air Force, greets Capt. Clark Gable at High Wycombe.

Gable was attached to the 351st Bomb Group on special assignment to make a training film about aerial gunners, May to September 1943. In the course of this duty he flew five combat missions, four with the 351st and one with the 303rd Bomb Group at Molesworth. He said that his greatest fear was that of being shot down and captured, expecting that Hitler would exhibit him in a cage. (USAAF)

▶ The dust rises from the Pierced Steel Plank surface as two 384th Fighter Squadron P-51Ds prepare to take off on runway 28, August 1944. (Mark Brown: Air Force Academy)

▼ A P-51D with only part of the 364th Fighter Group nose marking applied, seen on the 383rd Fighter Squadron dispersal within the perimeter track on the north side of the airfield and looking north towards the butts. (Mark Brown: Air Force Academy)

▼ Mechanics working on the Merlin engine of a 383rd Fighter Squadron Mustang on the same hardstand area as at left. The wheeled machine is a 'putt-putt' auxiliary starting unit, which was plugged into the aircraft's electrical system to boost the charge when the starter motor was operated. (Mark Brown: Air Force Academy)

▲ Refuelling a 383rd P-51D from an articulated 'gas wagon', the standard USAAF tanker vehicle for aviation gasoline. With a capacity of 4,000 US gallons, it could replenish between eight and ten P-51s per load. The wooden packing cases in the background held the aluminium 75 US gallon capacity 'drop tanks' used by this group. (Mark Brown: Air Force Academy)

HONINGTON/TROSTON STATION 595

1 SAD

▲ An unidentified B-17G taking off from runway 28, viewed from a point on the eastern end of the airfield looking south-west. The four C-type hangars dated from the construction of Honington in the 1930s; three were used by the 1st Strategic Air Depot for major overhaul, modification and repair of B-17s of the 3rd Division. (Mark Brown: Air Force Academy)

▲ *Sandy's Refuelling Boys*, with toilet roll emblem, was the slogan that adorned the right side of the nose on the 412th Bomb Squadron B-17 called *GI Issue: Government Property* (painted on the left side). One of the first Fortresses in natural metal finish received by the 95th Bomb Group, it was the only 8th Air Force bomber that failed to return from a mission to Stuttgart on 16 December 1944, the aircraft's 88th. There were no survivors. (Albert J. Keeler)

▼ The Dancisin crew typified the varied make-up of a bomber crew in the summer of 1944. The men flew 35 missions between April and August, usually in a B-17G named *Full House*. This aircraft was lost with another crew on 16 August 1944 and for this series of photos the Dancisin crew posed with *GI Issue* although they never flew a combat mission in this aircraft. Pilot 1/Lt George Dancisin (23) came from Bayonne, New Jersey, where he had worked in a zipper

factory before joining the USAAF. He was the only married member of the crew and a baby son was born while he was at Horham. 'Danny' had played some semi-pro football before the war and the crew liked to tease him about the great future he sacrificed for the Air Corps.

▼ Stocky 22 year-old 1/Lt Albert Keeler, co-pilot, wearing an A-2 flying jacket emblazoned with his record of operations and, on the right pocket, the insignia of *Full House*. He studied the violin for fourteen years and attended Ithaca College, New York, with the intention of becoming a music teacher until the outbreak of war. Later he flew in the Korean War and subsequently remained in the USAF.

► 1/Lt Foster Sherwood, bombardier, from Willis, Michigan was a slender, wiry, 'girl crazy' 22 year-old. He was killed in a flying accident post-war.

►► 1/Lt Frank Morrison (28), navigator, was short, stocky and stable and worked in the grain and feed business at Alpha, Minnesota, until being inducted into the US Army in March 1942. During a flight out of Poltava, Russia, in August 1944 his B-17 caught fire and he and the bombardier baled out. They then hitch-hiked by air via Poltava, Tehran, Cairo and Casablanca back to the UK to find that the rest of the crew had flown three more missions. In an effort to catch up, Morrison and Sherwood volunteered to fill vacancies on any crew but had only flown 33 when the rest of the Dancisan crew completed their 35th. After flying his 34th with another crew, during which the B-17 was badly shot up, Morrison was called to the Group CO's office, where Col Truesdale said, 'The way you're running into flak and fighters, do you want to call it a day and go home with the rest of your crew?' Morrison said he wasn't one to disagree with a colonel.

▶ S/Sgt Ray Rich (24), top turret gunner from Kensington, Connecticut, perched on the position he flew. There are no guns installed in the cooling barrels.

▼ T/Sgt Alyre Comeau, radio operator in the hatch above the radio room. Known as 'Joe' to the rest of the crew, Comeau was 20 years old and came from Madison, Maine. Of French Canadian descent, he had a strong New England accent.

▼ S/Sgt Leo Makelky, ball turret gunner, of slender build and happy disposition. Just 20 years old and from Mandon, North Dakota, he had worked for Douglas Aircraft for a year before enlisting in the AAF. Coming to the UK in April 1944, he returned the following September with a DFC and 35 missions 'under his belt'.

▲ S/Sgt Bob Rogers (19), right waist gunner from Pineville, Missouri, went straight from High School to the Air Corps. He was considered the joker of the crew. Here, as on all late-production B-17s, the waist windows are enclosed with Plexiglas to keep out the slipstream.

▲▶ T/Sgt Gordon Langford, left waist gunner and engineer, was, at 30, the 'old man' of the crew. His home town was Salt Lake City, Utah. A lanky individual, he was nicknamed 'Sack Time' because he slept a lot. Originally the flight engineer manned the top turret guns, being nearer to the equipment he had to monitor. However, it was difficult getting in and out of the top turret, apart from the danger of leaving an important defensive position.

▲▶ S/Sgt Larry Stevens, tail gunner from Alhambra, California, was 20, tall and of average build. Artistic talent found him painting the crew's flight jackets. Red was the squadron colour of the 412th and this form of marking was used in the 95th Bomb Group in place of, or in addition to, the fuselage identity letters. All these photographs were taken on hardstand No 47 on the west side of the airfield just behind Reading Hall Farm. (All individual crew member photos: Albert J. Keeler)

▼ Many US servicemen soon discovered that there were women in the locality of their bases who were pleased to earn a few shillings by doing laundry. The go-betweens were usually children, who were eager to undertake the task of fetching and carrying as they often benefited from the GIs' generosity with candy bars. Thirteen year-old Peter Brame, dressed in his Sunday best, was the laundry boy for the *Full House* crew and is here photographed on the 412th Bomb Squadron site, No 4. (Albert J. Keeler)

▼ Lt Col Harry G. Mumford in his jeep, August 1944. A member of the 95th's original air echelon, 'Grif' Mumford was CO of the 412th Bomb Squadron, Group Operations Officer and Group Air Executive. He was a distinguished officer and his chief claim to fame was being leader of the 95th Bomb Group formation that attacked Berlin on 4 March 1944 – the first occasion an 8th Air Force unit bombed the enemy capital. (Albert J. Keeler)

◄ A Fortress of the 335th Bomb Squadron rises from runway 25 on a sunny August Sunday in 1944. One of the wartime airfields on which construction began in 1941, Horham had its two hangars grouped together whereas later airfields usually had their hangars widely separated. (Albert J. Keeler)

► B-17G 'Neglect B-Baker' had opened its bomb bay doors more than 60 times to unload a lethal cargo. On this occasion food containers are about to fall on a dropping zone near Utrecht, Netherlands, 6 May 1945. The yellow nose band identifies the squadron of assignment as the 334th. Note the flooded countryside. (Mark Brown: Air Force Academy)

► *Liberty Lib* shot up and with wounded aboard near the hangar line apron at Horsham St Faith. The weight of several men entering the rear fuselage to assist was sufficient to bring the rear fuselage down on its skid and the nose wheel off the ground. This B-24H survived to the end of hostilities. (USAAF K2465)

▼ A three-plane 'vee' near the Norfolk coast, led by the 458th Bomb Group's second assembly ship, known as the *Spotted Ape*. The paint scheme was arguably the most eye-catching of all those applied to Liberators for the purpose of aiding mission formations. The aircraft was written off in a crash on 9 March 1945. The 753rd Bomb Squadron aircraft nearest the camera was equipped for the Azon mission, unique to this unit in the 8th Air Force. Individual bombs with a degree of directional control in

azimuth via an attached radio receiver were guided by the bombardier to a target. The three

aerials under the rear fuselage carried the transmitting signals. Named *SOL* (the initial letters of

an obscenity), this B-24J was withdrawn in November 1944. (USAAF K1147)

▼ A favourite subject for nose art was the female form. The young lady on *Top o' The Mark* appears quite unsuited for the '40 below' temperatures at which the bomber operated, to say nothing of the chill January day on which this picture was taken. Crew 22, 754th Bomb Squadron, all wear electrically heated flying suits. The two pilots have back-pack parachutes, the other seven members the quick-hitch chest type. The white scarves are made of parachute silk and serve to give warmth and stop chafing at the neck. (Richard M. Eselgroth)

▲ Take-off on runway 23, looking west towards the Cromer road. The winter of 1944–45 was unusually severe for England, prolonged periods of snow and frost making the servicing of aircraft in the open an extremely unpleasant task. (Richard M. Eselgroth)

► The 755th Bomb Squadron's *Hookem Cow* photographed in August 1944 on hardstand 11, looking north towards Horsham St Faith village and church. The aircraft crashed on take-off on 14 April 1945. (USAAF K2469)

► In the darkest days of the 8th Air Force's bomber offensive there were individual aircraft that inspired confidence in their crews. One was the 524th Bomb Squadron's *Paddy Gremlin*, received by the Squadron in June 1943 and apparently named by the ground crew. By August, when taken over by Lt Arvid O. Dahl's crew, this B-17F had already survived a few costly missions. The going was to get even tougher, for *Paddy Gremlin* took the Dahl crew to Schweinfurt and back safely on 17 August and again to the same target on the infamous 14 October mission. That day, when 60 B-17s were lost, *Paddy Gremlin* was one of only two 379th Bomb Group aircraft that landed back at Kimbolton – even if it was downwind. As its navigator, Lt Connie Anszperger, remarked, 'After that we all felt the plane had a charmed life.' *Paddy Gremlin* continued to evade the worst of flak and fighters. Then, on 30 January 1944, in the hands of Lt Kenneth Davis's crew, it was struck by a bomb dropped by an aircraft higher in the formation. With the No 3 engine crippled, and despite efforts to keep up with the formation, the bomber lost height and was eventually forced to crash-land near the Belgian border. The crew were unharmed until an enemy fighter strafed the aircraft, wounding two men seriously and six slightly. The

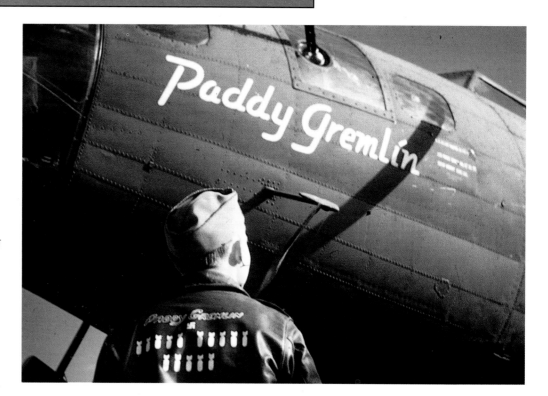

reason for this action was, the survivors believed, to prevent them setting fire to the wrecked aircraft. The photograph shows the navigator, Lt Constant Anszperger, with an A-2 jacket displaying fifteen missions in *Paddy Gremlin*. (Constant Anszperger)

▼ B-17F *Paddy Gremlin* on hardstand No 3 on the first loop cluster to the east of runway 21 bordering the railway line at Kimbolton. 'WA' identified the 524th Bomb Squadron; 'Y' was the individual plane-in-squadron letter and radio call ('Y-Yoke'); '23325'

was the concise version of the serial number, 42-3325; and the triangle was the 1st Bomb Division symbol and the blue 'K' therein the identification letter of the 379th Bomb Group. (Constant Anszperger)

▲ The novelty of being one of the first Fortresses in natural metal finish to be received by the 379th (in March 1944) is reflected in the name of this B-17, *Hi Ho Silver*. A few weeks after this photograph was taken, on 12 September 1944, the bomber received extensive damage as a result of a mid-air collision and had to be scrapped. (Robert Astrella)

◄ *The Wish Bone* flew 88 missions with the 526th Bomb Squadron before wear and tear forced its retirement. Operational training duties followed, and by the end of the war its Olive Drab camouflage had faded to a light purplish brown shade, contrasting with the green applied to re-worked areas. (Arnold N. Delmonico)

▼ The shiny metal repair patches bear witness to the damage wrought by enemy fire. This B-17G was destroyed in a crash and the crew killed while low-flying over a town on 8 July 1944. (Edmund H. Lutz)

▶ A crew chief talks with Capt. Donald H. McAuley in *Pistol Packin' Mama* after this 55th Fighter Squadron pilot's return from his first combat sortie, 1 December 1943. The photograph was taken at Nuthampstead, where selected pilots of the 20th Fighter Group had their combat mission initiation flying with the 55th Fighter Group. 'Mac' McAuley took command of the 55th Fighter Squadron in March 1944 but went missing in action on 23 April that year, his Lightning being hit by ground fire during a strafing attack on Chateaudun airfield in France. McAuley was reported to have baled out but it was subsequently learnt that he had died of wounds. *Pistol Packin' Mama*, in common with most 8th Air Force P-38Hs, was sent to the warmer climate of the Mediterranean theatre in February 1944. (Air Force Museum)

◀ Cpl Carl Barlow with a belt of .50-calibre ammunition for the CO's P-38J, June 1944. *Wrangler* was the personal 'mount' of Lt Col Cy Wilson, commanding the 55th Fighter Squadron at the date of this photograph, who was soon to become CO of the 20th Fighter Group. He went missing in action in a Mustang during August that year, being captured and imprisoned at Stalag Luft I. (John W. Phegley)

▼ Lt Richard O. Loehnert's *California Cutie*, June 1944, sports the yellow propeller spinners that identified the 20th Fighter Group's Lightnings at this time. The white band and polished metal nose scheme was intended to make it difficult for the enemy to tell whether a P-38 was an armed aircraft or an unarmed, glazed-nose version. The various symbols for actions are: top hat and cane for bomber escorts; umbrellas for top-cover support; brooms for fighter sweeps; bombs for fighter-bomber attacks; and locomotives for those claimed destroyed by strafing. The white cross marks the aircraft's centre of gravity. The armourer is cleaning the .50-calibre machine gun barrels. (John W. Phegley)

▶ The ground crew working on *Wrangler*, late June 1944. At this time the P-38's fuselage booms were still adorned with black and white 'D-Day' markings. For several weeks following the Normandy landings, Lightning units in particular were tasked with beach-head patrolling as their distinctive configuration could easily be judged by anti-aircraft gunners to be that of a friendly aircraft. (John W. Phegley)

▲ Part of the 55th Fighter Squadron dispersal area, late June 1944. One mechanic surveys the 150 US gallon capacity 'drop tanks' that were the standard fitment on Lightnings to extend their range. The P-38J under maintenance, 42-104207, was lost on 16 July 1944 in the Channel not far from Margate. The pilot, 1/Lt John Klink, was nursing the aircraft home on one engine when that suddenly failed and he had to bale out. The RAF Air–Sea Rescue service responded to his 'May Day' call and Klink was picked up little the worse for his ducking. (John W. Phegley)

◀ Capt. Jack Ilfrey, Operations Officer of the 79th Fighter Squadron in July 1944, posing on his P-51D *Happy Jack's Go Buggy*. 'Happy Jack' first came to the UK with the 1st Fighter Group, going on to North Africa where he became its first ace. He was sent to the 20th Fighter Group to increase its experience level and his final 'score' of enemy aircraft was eight, all downed while flying P-38s. Taking command of the Squadron, he continued combat flying until December 1944. His total combat hours were 548, of which 320 were from the UK. (John Hudgen)

◄ Knettishall was only a few miles from the small town of Thetford, which, 388th Bomb Group personnel soon discovered, was the birthplace of Thomas Paine, who served in the American Army during the War of Independence. It was decided to name a replacement B-17F, received by the 562nd Bomb Squadron in September 1943, in his honour and the town dignataries were invited to participate in a ceremony that was basically an exercise in promoting Anglo-American goodwill. Some saw it as rather insensitive, for while Tom Paine might be a son of Thetford, he could be considered a British traitor. The aircraft was retired from combat operations in the spring of 1944. (USAAF: K3973)

▼ Bound for tactical targets around Brest on 26 August 1944, the 561st Bomb Squadron's *Lotta Bull* flies left wing on the high squadron lead. Lt R. Gladstone's crew were in charge on this occasion. The 'H' of the Group's identity marking on the tail has a high bar – a feature, common to all 388th B-17s, which often caused the 'H' to be mistaken for an 'M' at distance. The 388th

was the only group in 8th Air Force that had no squadron identity markings of any kind on its B-17s. A few days after this photograph was taken, while the aircraft was returning with another crew on another mission over France in heavy cloud, loss of instrumentation apparently caused the pilots to become disorientated and the B-17 stalled out and spun. The crew parachuted safely. Gladstone's crew were on their 32nd mission when their aircraft blew up after being hit by flak. Only one man lived. (Mark Brown: Air Force Academy)

► The Group lead aircraft, after a mission to Brest, nearing home base. Equipped with H2X ground scanning radar, this aircraft was assigned to the 96th Bomb Group's 413th Bomb Squadron, which provided pathfinder services for the 388th at this date. As the aircraft usually operated in support of the 388th and with a 388th crew detached to the pathfinder squadron, the Group marking was carried on tail and wing. This B-17 was destroyed by an engine fire at Snetterton Heath in March 1945. (Mark Brown: Air Force Academy)

▲ Back at its dispersal point adjacent to the technical site, *Miss Fortune* of the 561st Bomb Squadron is looked over by its ground crew and refuelled. The photographer flew in this B-17G on the Brest mission. Misfortune finally befell the aircraft on 6 February 1945 when, while gaining formation for a mission, it collided with a 490th Bomb Group B-17 in heavy cloud over Cambridgeshire and crashed at Wicken. All the crew baled out but the co-pilot was killed when his parachute failed to open. This photograph was taken looking north of west towards the control tower. (Mark Brown: Air Force Academy)

► Crossing the threshold of runway 27 for landing: a view through the nose with covered bomb sight, chin turret sight and operating arm in the foreground. This runway had a pronounced dip in the middle, just discernible in the picture. The technical site can be seen on the left, as also can Elms Farm, Alpheton. (Mark Brown: Air Force Academy)

◄ Another view through the nose of a B-17 taxying back through the dispersal area on the north-west side of the airfield, looking north-east. The perimeter track was 50 feet wide, the Fortress's wing span 103 feet. The yellow tail and wing tips identified the 4th Combat Wing, of which the 487th was a part. The red and yellow chevron on the right wing identified the Group within the Wing. (Mark Brown: Air Force Academy)

▲ A B-17G of the 839th Bomb Squadron named *Our Baby*, on its way to shower fire bombs (napalm) on the isolated *Wehrmacht* defensive positions at Royan that were preventing the use of Bordeaux as a port. The photograph is dated 15 April 1945. (Mark Brown: Air Force Academy)

▼ The low squadron of the 487th Bomb Group formation over France on 15 April 1945. (Mark Brown: Air Force Academy)

► Lt Harvey F. Mace of the 362nd Fighter Squadron stands in front of his P-51B, named *Sweet Helen* after his wife. This photograph was taken in front of a blister hangar south of the southernmost T2 hangar, about March 1944. There were a dozen 'blisters' on this airfield for the covered repair of fighter aircraft. The view is to the west, with Hill Farm in the background. At this time the 357th Fighter Group had still to adopt the red and yellow chequerboard group marking. Harvey Mace wears the popular RAF flying boots, which were more secure in bale-outs than the US types and also became a 'walking shoe' (the tops could be cut off) if there were an opportunity to evade capture. (Harvey F. Mace)

▼ Photographed here while visiting Steeple Morden in the spring of 1945, *Butch Baby* was the personal Mustang of Maj. Joseph Broadhead, CO of the 362nd Fighter Squadron. Delivered in bare metal finish, this was one of several 357th Fighter Group Mustangs given a dress of Olive Green and grey in case the unit were moved to airfields on the Continent after D-Day. The bare metal patch on the fin carries the

antenna of the tail warning radar. The device, designated AN/APS-13, gave a pilot both visual and audible warning in the cockpit of the approach of another aircraft from the rear, up to four miles distant. Joe Broadhead was an original member of the 357th Fighter Group and was credited with the destruction of eight enemy aircraft in the air. (Alexander C. Sloan)

▶ Harvey Mace's second Mustang, a P-51D christened *Sweet Helen II*, as seen looking north towards the Theberton conifer woods, about July 1944. Mace flew this aircraft on the 'shuttle' to Russia in August 1944; he also claimed two air victories while flying this P-51D. The 'drop tanks' under the wings are the British-made steel 108 US gallon type. (Harvey F. Mace)

◀ The name *Frisco Kid* acknowledged pilot Lt John C. Casey's home city. This photograph was taken at Eye. (Arnold N. Delmonico)

▶ *Li'l Kitten*, a P-51B assigned to Lt Louis Fechet, was received by the 357th Fighter Group in natural metal finish and given a camouflage coat at Leiston. When this photograph was taken late in October 1944, propeller slipstream had by then whipped up so much 'dirt' on landing grounds that the blast had removed most of the paint from the lower parts of the fuselage. The P-51B was a much nicer aircraft to handle than the P-51D but it lacked firepower, having only four against the latter's six guns. The restricted view from the cockpit led to the fitting of bulged, British-made Malcolm hoods. (Robert Astrella)

◄ The Chevrolet Runway Control Truck used by the 361st Fighter Group, with a windsock and a high-visibility flag on attached masts. The structure over the controller's position afforded some degree of weather protection. Posing for the camera is Lt J. D. Smith, a 376th Fighter Squadron pilot, on duty shift as Assistant Operations Officer for his unit. Jim Smith flew his first combat mission on D-Day, having arrived from a training establishment only the day before, 5 June 1944. (James D. Smith)

► The control tower at Little Walden, viewed to the north-west from the perimeter track, was to the design common to most bomber airfields built to Class A standard. Constructed of brick and with a concrete rendering, it housed Flying Control and the Weather Office. The large placards carry the number of the runway in use at that time, 04 being the south-west/north-east runway. The masts on roof are for measuring wind speeds and direction. The vehicle is a crash truck, always on hand to go to the scene of any aircraft coming to grief near the airfield. (James D. Smith)

▲ Tails lift as two Mustangs of the 375th Fighter Squadron take off from runway 04, December 1944. The nearest aircraft to the photographer on the control tower is Lt Bill Kemp's *Betty Lee III*. (James D. Smith)

▲ The Roll of Honor in the 376th Fighter Squadron Ready Room at Little Walden, showing the names of those pilots who had been killed during the unit's first ten months of combat. Of the fifteen named, four pilots were killed in action over enemy territory, six were taken prisoner, one evaded capture and returned to the UK and four were killed in accidents in the UK. (James D. Smith)

◄ The Cessna UC-78 Bobcat utility transport assigned to group headquarters and named *Uncle Tom's Cabin*, probably after the original Group commander, Col Tom Christian. Largely of canvas and wood construction, the UC-78 had weaknesses, which, because of a number of fatal accidents, led to flight restrictions. Lt Victor Bocquin, another 376th fighter pilot, leans on the yellow cowlings denoting 361st Group ownership. (James D. Smith)

► High over the Continent, Lt Robert Schmidt heads home to Martlesham. The Mustang was inherited from Capt. John W. Crump who had completed his tour. Schmidt had the nickname *Jackie* removed and the aircraft renamed *Tar Heel* after his home state. (Robert Schmidt)

▲ At some 30,000 feet on an escort mission over Germany, Lt Clifford Poppell's P-51D *Barbara* hugs two 108 US gallon drop tanks. (Herbert R. Rutland)

► Off-duty fighter pilot: Lt Herb Rutland poses on a 360th Fighter Squadron Mustang. He wears a B-10 olive flight jacket with mouton collar, a smart and popular garment among the fraternity. Rutland joined the unit in January 1945 but, like most newcomers at that stage in the war, had little opportunity to engage the enemy in air combat before the end of hostilities. His comment on shooting up the enemy airfields: 'I just hope I scared the enemy as much as I did myself'. (Herbert R. Rutland)

▲ Heading for the rendezvous with bombers, two P-51s of the 360th Fighter Squadron, spread in battle formation, pass through contrails made by other escort fighters deep in Germany, about March 1945. (Herbert R. Rutland)

► Most 8th Air Force personnel had a humble Nissen hut for their quarters but the pilots of the 360th Fighter Squadron had an Elizabethan mansion! Martlesham Heath could not accommodate a whole US fighter group, so the 359th and 360th Squadrons were placed in Kesgrave and Playford Halls, two very large country houses close to the airfield. (Herbert R. Rutland)

► *Betta Duck*, a B-24J of the 7th Bomb Squadron coming in for a landing, shows stress ripples in the fuselage skin. When the 34th converted to Fortresses, *Betta Duck* was sent to serve with the 466th Bomb Group at Attlebridge, where it saw out the war, and was subsequently returned to the US. (Robert Astrella)

▼ Devoid of name and other unofficial decorations, this 18th Bomb Squadron B-24H was lost in distressing circumstances – a collision with another B-24 in the formation. This occurred on 19 July 1944 during a mission to Saarbrücken. Both Liberators went down, with 21 crew members listed as MIA. (Robert Astrella)

► Work on a 7th Bomb Squadron Fortress in No 1 hangar on the main technical site. The T2 type hangar was standard on the wartime constructed bomber airfields, there being three or four on those completed in 1942 and usually only two on the later airfields. The T2 was approximately 240 feet long by 115 feet wide and could accommodate three B-17s or B-24s. Its basic construction consisted of a steel portal frame, with corrugated sheet steel cladding. Most were painted black but this one has received a coat of matt camouflage green. On the right of the south-west door of the hangar are replacement B-17 tailplane and wing sections and on the left a so-called Weapons Carrier vehicle. The pole supports a tannoy loud speaker, one of several placed around the base to broadcast messages from the control tower – including air raid alerts. (Mark Brown: Air Force Academy)

► Engine change on an 18th Bomb Squadron B-17G on dispersal point No 11 (the 34th Bomb Group renumbered all its hardstand parking from the original system). The removed engine is to the right and a mechanic prepares the new one which is held by a crane hoist. A Wright R-1820 engine weighed approximately 1200lb and had an average life of 300 hours before major overhaul. Engine change time varied, but the job usually took around five hours. (Mark Brown: Air Force Academy)

▼► A view from a 7th Bomb Squadron B-17G's top turret of other Squadron aircraft returning from the food drop to the people of Utrecht, May 1945. The nearest aircraft is *No Gum Chum*, a name derived from the persistent request to GIs from English children for chewing gum. A yellow nose band and propeller bosses identify the 7th Bomb Squadron; the red forward part of the tail fin denotes the 34th Bomb Group. *No Gum Chum* was involved in an incident illustrating the dangers of flying at high altitudes if there were problems with the oxygen system. Navigator 'Bud' Pochter relates what occurred on 25 November 1944 as the B-17 was heading for Merseberg at 26,000 feet:

'We had been on our way almost three hours and I had just called an oxygen check only minutes before, with all positions reporting OK. Then, without warning, we went into a steep dive. The crew throughout the aircraft began shouting on the intercom, wondering what was happening. I left my navigator's position in the nose and dived down under the front hatch to get up to the flight deck. The sight made me gulp. Our top turret gunner was slumped unconscious on the floor and my pilot and co-pilot were desperately trying to link themselves to an auxiliary oxygen line. A glance at the gauge showed their normal system to be empty. I quickly reached for other auxiliary oxygen lines and gave one to each. We were

still going down and approaching 300mph, but I could see the oxygen had revived the pilots and they were attempting to bring the plane out of the dive. I reconnected my intercom and shouted to the crew that we would be under control and not to bale out. We eventually levelled off at 9,000ft.

'I quickly examined our top turret gunner. He was still unconscious and his skin colour was deep blue, indicating that he was suffering severe anoxia – lack of oxygen. Other crew members appeared and we began emergency first aid. Our pilot reminded me that he had informed the group leader we were aborting and he needed a course heading back to

base. My mind filled with concern for our gunner; the shortest route back to base was given, even though this meant overflying enemy coast positions at low altitude. We did draw some ground fire and despite the unsettled weather lost little time in reaching Mendlesham. An ambulance was racing alongside as we landed and the gunner was rushed to hospital.

'The pilot and I had to file a report to explain the reason for aborting the mission. The ground crew checked all oxygen systems and *none leaked*! The top brass was not happy and wanted an explanation. We entered the aircraft, carefully examining the flight deck and top turret. Out of

curiosity I climbed into the turret, turned on the power switches and began to turn it around. All of a sudden there was a hissing sound and in moments the oxygen gauge showed zero. We investigated the sound and discovered a flak hole in the line going to the turret. Only when the turret was in a certain position would it leak. Since pilot, co-pilot and top gunner all used the same system, the rotation had allowed the leak to occur and hence our misfortune. We were relieved to find the cause, but regretted the accident to our crew member. He did survive but was confined to military hospitals for the remainder of his life.' (Mark Brown: Air Force Academy)

◄ One of the 23 Douglas Boston IIIs supplied to the 8th Air Force by the RAF in August 1942 to equip the 15th Bomb Squadron at Molesworth. This was the unit that, on 4 July that year, undertook the first USAAF bombing operation from the UK using an RAF squadron's Bostons. AL452 remained in the UK when the 15th Bomb Squadron moved to North Africa in November 1942, subsequently serving in communication duties with the 1st Bomb Division until the end of the war. The aircraft remained 'F for Freddie' throughout its near-three years of 8th Air Force service. (USAAF)

MOLESWORTH

303 BG
358/359/360/427 BS

► Positioning for the lead of a combat wing, the 303rd Bomb Group formation climbs over England, 16 March 1944. This view from a Fortress in the higher 379th Bomb Group reveals the three-plane elements with which group formations were built. (Edmund H. Lutz)

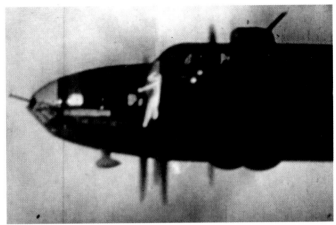

▲ Withdrawn from the 359th Bomb Squadron at the end of March 1944 for return to the US, these two B-17Fs were at the time the oldest operational Fortresses in the 8th Air Force. *Black Diamond Express* (left) had originally been intended for the RAF but came to the UK with the 92nd Bomb Group and entered combat with the 97th Bomb Group in 1942. Assigned to the 303rd Bomb Group in the spring of 1943, this venerable bomber was involved in many of the great air battles of that year. *The Duchess* (right) was famous as the Fortress in which bombardier Jack Mathis earned a posthumous Medal of Honor on 18 March 1943, the first award of the highest US decoration for bravery to go to an 8th Air Force flier. (USAAF)

MOUNT FARM
OXFORDSHIRE • STATION 234

7 PG
13/14/22/27 PS

▶ *The Florida Gator*, with eleven camera-toting sorties to its credit. Tended by S/Sgt J. C. Ginex, this F-5C was lost near St-Malo on 24 July 1944 with Lt Edward W. Durst who, it is believed, succumbed to anoxia. The camera port is ahead of the undercarriage leg. (Robert Astrella)

► Another F-5C photographic version of the Lightning fighter, *Ginger Snap* has a somewhat buxom version of a popular Varga calendar girl illustration. (Robert Astrella)

▼ Photo technicians installing a K-17 camera in the nose compartment of F-5E 44-24225 of the 22nd Photo Squadron on a hardstanding at the south-east corner of the airfield. This picture was taken, looking west, early in 1945 when the 7th Photo Group had standardized on identification markings consisting of a deep blue spinner and a red cowling stripe to denote the Group and a white rudder to identify the 22nd Photo Squadron. (Robert Astrella)

▲ A new F-5E resplendent in the colours of 'A' Flight, 13th Photo Squadron, reposing on a Pierced Steel Plank standing situated on the northern side of the airfield, viewed looking east, about July 1944. (Robert Astrella)

◀ The same aircraft later that year, now named *Lanakila* and with 41 sorties to its credit. At this time its assigned pilot was Lt Albert Clark, who was shot down by fighters in another F-5 on 9 August 1944 and made prisoner. (Robert Astrella)

▲ The 8th Air Force's only long-term B-25C Mitchell arrived in the UK in March 1943, when it was still planned to send combat groups with this type to the European theatre. The aircraft was subsequently used for communications work but in August 1944 flew thirteen night photographic sorties over V-weapon sites along the Channel coast. Thereafter all the paint was removed and *Miss Nashville* appeared in polished bare metal. The aircraft was written off in France on 26 October 1944 after being hit by anti-aircraft artillery fire while on a courier mission. The photograph was taken about September 1944. (Robert Astrella)

◄ One of the first Spitfire XI photographic reconnaissance aircraft to be based at Mount Farm, MB950 weathered fifteen months of operations before being returned to the RAF at the end of March 1945. Unarmed and fast, these aircraft were used chiefly for the deepest penetrations of enemy airspace to obtain target assessment photographs. While not as comfortable as, and noisier than, the F-5 Lightnings, the Spitfires impressed with their low mechanical failure rate. They also required only a third of the servicing time needed for the F-5. (Robert Astrella)

▲ Two Spitfires of Yellow Flight have their engines run up while PA841 stands wrapped up for the night. This photograph was taken in October 1944 on the north-west pan hardstand at the north-east corner of the airfield, looking west towards a 14th Photo Squadron maintenance hangar. (Robert Astrella)

▼ Spitfire dispersal at Mount Farm, about October 1944: 'gassing up' PA914 from a 2,500 gallon tanker on an Autocar tractor unit. The other Spitfire has a 'putt-putt' battery booster plugged in and ready to operate. (Robert Astrella)

◄ PL914 is run up while ground crewmen hold down the tail and others steady the wings. (Robert Astrella)

▼ Gassing up MB946 of White Flight, 14th Photo Squadron, about October 1944. This Spitfire carries 52 symbols for completed combat sorties at this time. The crew chief was Sgt Kinder. (Robert Astrella)

▼ Spitfire XI PA842 takes off from runway 30 past a parked Cessna UC-78 Bobcat, about March 1945. By this date the Spitfires' original PRU blue paint had been removed and they were operating in bare metal finish. The aircraft also has the green rudder that identified the 14th Photo Squadron. PA842, along with most of the Squadron's Spitfires, was returned to the RAF at the end of this month. (Robert Astrella)

◄ The comparatively high losses of F-5 Lightnings to *Luftwaffe* interceptors, particularly to Me 262 jets, led to the provision of a number of P-51 Mustangs so that the 7th Photo Group could fly its own escorts for photographic reconnaissance sorties. This aircraft, a P-51K assigned to the 22nd Photo Squadron, is taxying on the eastern perimeter track to the head of runway 30, about March 1945. The Mustang has the Group's red cowling stripe and blue spinner. The mobile airfield beacon for night signalling can be seen at the right. (Robert Astrella)

◄ Against a threatening sky, the Group's AT-6D Texan, 42-85066, prepares to take off from runway 35. The green paintwork on the cowling was apparently inherited from a previous user. (Robert Astrella)

► A veteran F-5B, *Tough Kid*, was showing signs of wear when this photograph was taken early in 1945. The access panel around the oblique-facing camera port no longer fits snugly because of the number of times it had been removed and replaced. Note the nose camera port, which normally concealed a K-17 camera. (Robert Astrella)

492 BG

▶ A comic motif on a B-24J from an organization which had an unenviable distinction in that (to quote historian Alan Blue) 'no other bombardment group in US history ever lost as many airplanes in combat in so short a time'. *Boulder Buff*'s crew was one of the more fortunate of the 52 to go down during the brief operational period of the 492nd Bomb Group in daylight bombing, May to August 1944. On 6 July this Liberator was hit in No 1 engine by flak over Kiel. The propeller could not be feathered and 'ran away', causing the aircraft to go into an uncontrollable left-hand dive – narrowly missing the bombs dropped by part of the 492nd formation – until the engine finally seized up. Lt Robert M. Munson and his co-pilot managed to get the aircraft into level flight but, finding themselves alone and having difficulty in maintaining height, they prudently sought sanctuary in neutral Sweden. A successful landing was made at Bulltofta, where the aircraft was photographed in company with

other Allied aircraft that had reached this haven. The B-24 in the immediate background is the 448th

Bomb Group's 42-51079 that arrived on 20 June 1944. (Air Force Museum)

NORTH PICKENHAM

491 BG

▼ Although *Tubarao* had only flown twenty combat missions in six months, wear and tear saw it declared War Weary (hence the 'WW' on the tail fin) and employed

as the Group's assembly ship. The previous aircraft used for this purpose had crashed after take-off in a snowstorm on 5 January 1945. Similar yellow and green striping to

that carried by the fallen B-24 was applied to make the aircraft conspicuous. The Liberator's nose shape lent itself to animated decoration, with the two

navigator's side windows becoming 'eyes' and the bombardier's outlook the 'mouth'. This photograph was taken at Mount Farm, about March 1945. (Robert Astrella)

▶ Fog was a feature of many winter days. Here a P-38H of the 38th Fighter Squadron is 'run up' in the mists that kept all aircraft on the ground, 26 December 1943. (Robert Sand)

◀ The 38th Fighter Squadron propeller crew working on P-38J 42-67904 'CG:O'. They are, left to right, T/Sgt Harold Melby, Cpl Merle Stivason, Sgt Robert Sand and S/Sgt Kermit Riem. The Curtiss propellers, with electrically controlled blade pitch actuation, were prone to troubles, particularly in the damp English climate. (Robert Sand)

▶ Thanksgiving Day, 25 November 1943, on the Communal Site looking east towards the airfield technical area: the enlisted men 'stand in line' for the traditional turkey dinner. Sgt Robert Sand, the photographer, observed: 'The newsreels were telling of the GIs getting a pound of turkey apiece. There were so few turkeys the officers donated all they had to the enlisted men. Seven turkeys, I believe. The cooks valiantly tried to feed 1,500 men by shredding the turkeys, including skin and even an occasional feature, and making a sort of cream hash. On the side was a huge helping of boiled navy beans. We felt sorry about taking the turkey from the officers but later were told they made out okay on steak. If true, steak just isn't Thanksgiving.' As can be seen, there was no shortage of mud at Nuthampstead. (Robert Sand)

► The 'flying wolf' design adopted by Maj. Milton Joel, CO of the 38th Fighter Squadron, as his personal insignia was rendered by Sgt Sand on P-38H 42-67020. Eleven days after this photograph was taken Joel was shot down during an escort to Bremen – as were six other members of the 55th Fighter Group. (Robert Sand)

▲ A display of rear ends: ground crew men examine one of the first P-38J models to arrive at Nuthampstead, December 1943. The shearling sheepskin jackets and trousers worn were essential to keep out the English winter chill that made life so uncomfortable for mechanics. (Robert Sand)

► Squadron painter of the 38th Fighter Squadron, Sgt Julius Cooper, 'known for his great laugh that preceeded him everywhere', applies camouflage green to the upper surfaces of a new, unpainted P-38J, 11 April 1944. A few days later the 55th Fighter Group left Nuthampstead for Wormingford. (Robert Sand)

◄ The high squadron leaves its mark in the sub-stratosphere. The hot exhaust fumes mixing with the high-humidity cold air formed the vapour trails. Relatively small changes in altitude would often extinguish these white markers – which frequently aided the enemy interceptors in locating the attacking bombers. (Robert Welty)

◄ Far above an undercast, the 603rd Bomb Squadron's *Kitty Kay* gleams in the afternoon sun. This Fortress was the only aircraft lost during a mission to Oranienburg on 15 March 1945. (Robert Welty)

► Stepped up, stepped down: 398th Bomb Group B-17s heading towards hostile airspace. The trail in the distance was made by a V-2 rocket going the other way. (Robert Welty)

◄ A pathfinder B-17G, 44-8553 of the 602nd Bomb Squadron, with radome (containing the H2X ground scanner) extended and bomb doors open on approach to Munster's rail marshalling yards, 26 October 1944. The plume of smoke is from an oil target being attacked by another group. (Robert Welty)

► Lt Robert Welty crouching over the retractable H2X radar scanner. Signals were fed to a 'scope' for the radar operator situated in the radio room – through the door in the next compartment. This is a late model Fortress: the aircraft has glazed waist gun windows and is unpainted internally. (Robert Welty)

◄ Another 'PFF ship' (pathfinder aircraft equipped with H2X) on target approach. This is a B-17G of the 601st Bomb Squadron. (Robert Welty)

▼ The rising sun silhouettes the tail of a Fortress. A patch can be seen on the Plexiglas window of the Cheyenne type gun position. Fortunately the gunner had his head turned away to check his oxygen regulator when the flak fragment that necessitated the patch sliced through. (Robert Welty)

◀ A wintry scene, with *Whiskey Jingles* taxying along the north side perimeter track: a photograph taken from hardstand No 14, looking north towards the bomb store and Besthorpe. This B-24H was assigned to the 735th Bomb Squadron and has the yellow propeller bosses that identified its unit within the Group. (Clyde Colvin)

▶ Liberators of the 735th Bomb Squadron returning from a mission. The camouflaged aircraft was unnamed at this time, late 1944, but became *Liberty Run* when it was chosen to carry a load of Christmas gifts donated by GIs to the children of liberated Paris. Note the white propeller boss on No 4 engine of the aircraft carrying the photographer. (Clyde Colvin)

▼ *Dorothy*, another 735th Bomb Squadron Liberator, on hardstand No 13, photographed in January 1945 looking north-east. The covers over the nose turret and top turret obviated the tedious job of removing frost before a flight. (Clyde Colvin)

▶ Its name a play on words, *Never Mrs* may not have missed the target but on 11 November 1944 the flak put up over the Bottrop oil refinery did not miss this B-24H. Lt John H Friedhaber and his crew were the only men missing from those in the force of 482 bombers despatched that day. This aircraft had completed 45 missions when the photograph was taken. (Kaylor C. Whitehead)

▶ A general view of *Never Mrs* on its dispersal point 7, to the east of the end of runway 21 on the northern side of the airfield. For most of her combat career this aircraft served Lt Kaylor Whitehead and crew. (Clyde Colvin)

▶ Mechanics at work on *Jennie*, a B-17F of the 510th Bomb Squadron, summer 1943. Assigned to the unit in May 1943, this bomber was shot down on its 31st mission by flak near Bordeaux on the last day of the same year. All the crew members survived as PoWs. (USAAF).

▶▼ The flaming wreckage of a Fortress near Hemington House, 7 May 1943, resulting from a collision between two B-17Fs returning from a practice mission. Both crews were killed. The airfield butts and a taxying B-17 can be seen in the distance. (USAAF)

▼ Ashton Wold House, the grand mansion to the north of the airfield in the grounds of which several base living sites were situated. It was and is the home of the Hon. Miriam Lane and is part of the Rothschild estates which included the site of Polebrook airfield. (Thomas L. Cooper)

▶ The anti-aircraft defences around the Politz oil plant were formidable – as the 351st Bomb Group found out on 7 October 1944. The Group formation did a single orbit in the target area in order to bomb visually but this probably allowed the *Luftwaffe*'s radars to give the flak gunners the necessary data for putting up an accurate barrage. Three B-17s were shot down and four others, badly damaged with little chance of returning to England, sought haven in neutral Sweden. These included the lead Fortress piloted by Lt Arthur Bartzocas with Lt Col Benoid Glawe as formation commander. Flak put two engines out of action and caused a serious fuel tank leak. Little of this damage shows in the photograph taken at Sovde where the aircraft landed. A pathfinder aircraft (H2X radome in place of ball turret) of the 509th Bomb Squadron, it was returned to the UK in May 1945. (Air Force Museum)

POYNTON
CHESHIRE • STATION 571

2 ADG

▶ A mural on the wall of the recreation hall used by the 2nd Air Depot Group, presenting a cartoon characterization of the United States. The artist was Sgt Tony Lipsky, to whom many base personnel offered suggestions to aid the expression of individual state symbols. The 2nd Air Depot Group, handling a vast variety of supply items, was the first major unit of the 8th Air Force to arrive in the UK.

◄ 'Between these gates pass the hottest damn flyers in the ETO' is the boast on the practice bomb elevated as a sign at the entrance to Site No 1. Originally No 5 when the camp was constructed, this site was renumbered by the 467th when it moved in and was used as the Administrative area. The men on the right are reading the latest additions to the base notice board. Apart from regulations and general orders, the board carried more pleasurable information such as the time and date of movie shows, dances and concerts. This is a view along the south entry road looking north. (John H. Seward)

▼ The 467th Bomb Group's 'assembly ship', *Pete the POM Inspector*, on hardstanding No 3, viewed looking west, in the summer of 1944. The name was derived from the 'P-Peter' identity letter of the 467th and the experience of the Post Overseas Movement Inspection prior to the Group's leaving the US. The requirement of being 'put in order'

applied to the task of the 'assembly ship' in establishing and monitoring formations. A B-24D, this aircraft originally served the 389th Bomb Group at Hethel as *Heaven Can Wait* before retirement from combat use. It was written off after a landing accident in late October 1944 when the nose wheel could not be lowered. (John H Seward)

► *Witchcraft*, a B-24H of the 790th Bomb Squadron, completed more combat missions without an 'abort' (an abandonment through mechanical or personnel failure) than any other Liberator in the 8th Air Force. The achievement was due in large measure to the dedication and care of the ground crew who serviced and maintained this aircraft, notably crew chief S/Sgt Joe Ramirez. In the 130 missions between 10 April 1944 and 21 April 1945, *Witchcraft* delivered 500,000lb of bombs and flew 665 combat hours. More than 300 flak holes were repaired and thirteen engine changes were made; on

three occasions the bomber was brought home on three engines. (James H Mahoney)

▼ The nose insignia of the 'assembly ship' with the officer keeping his eye on the scene

through a telescope. After this B-24D was withdrawn, another War Weary Liberator was painted up in similar livery (and with the same name) for formation assembly work. (John H. Seward)

▶ A 708th Bomb Squadron B-17G with bomb doors open on target approach, late 1944. (Clark B. Rollins)

▼ Damage to *A Bit o' Lace*, 4 April 1945, the result of a bursting flak shell over Kiel which riddled the tail fin and removed a large part of the left stabilizer and elevator. The smiling aviator is Sgt Clarence Walker, the tail gunner from Little Rock, Arkansas, known to the rest of his crew as 'Arkie' for the obvious reason. (John H. Kirkwood)

◀ A view of the Lead B-17 from the Deputy Lead on the run from the Initial Point to target at Plauen, 8 April 1945. The camouflaged aircraft beyond the Lead ship is *Scheherazade*, a veteran 709th Bomb Squadron Fortress which had flown more than 100 combat missions. This photograph was taken using an Argos 35mm camera, set to 1/100th of a second and at a range of 100 feet. (John H. Kirkwood)

► A low-altitude drop to the French Maquis in Operation 'Grassy' on 9 September 1944. This 708th Bomb Squadron Fortress has just released parachute containers, one of which can be seen unfolding close under the tail. (Mark Brown: Air Force Academy)

◄ The damaged vertical tail surfaces of *A Bit o' Lace* after the 4 April mission. 'Flak patches' over perforations received on an earlier occasion show in the aircraft's number and the Group insignia, but this time a complete change of tail surfaces was necessary. The sheet metal men who did the patch riveting were at times some of the busiest people on a bomber base. (John H. Kirkwood)

▲ Another Fortress releasing parachute containers over a location 25 miles south of Besançon in the Massif Central. The 710th Bomb Squadron aircraft has its landing gear lowered to reduce airspeed. Although these drops of arms and ammunition to the French Resistance movement were made far behind enemy lines, there were no losses to the B-17s involved. (Mark Brown: Air Force Academy)

◄ The 447th Bomb Group's veteran *Cock o' the Sky* on hardstand No 9, spring 1945. Red engine cowlings were the 710th Bomb Squadron's identification marking. The small 'garden huts' in the background were used by ground crews to shelter and protect equipment from inclement weather. (Mark Brown: Air Force Academy)

◄ Though hardly an appropriate name for an instrument of war, *Dove of Peace* was the inscription applied to all Col Glenn Duncan's personal fighter aircraft. This is the last and eighth of that name, photographed while on a visit to Thorpe Abbotts in the spring of 1945. Glenn Duncan, an 'ace' credited with shooting down nineteen enemy aircraft, was himself shot down by ground fire on 7 July 1944 but successfully evaded capture by being hidden by the Dutch Underground for several months. The yellow and black chequerboard of the 353rd vied with those in black and white of the 78th Fighter Group as the most eye-catching identification markings of all 8th Air Force fighter groups. (100th BG Memorial Museum)

RIDGEWELL
ESSEX • STATION 167

381 BG
532/533/534/535 BS

▼ *Patches* (nearest camera) and *Sleepy Time Gal* of the 532nd Bomb Squadron in flight over East Anglia, about September 1944.

Patches, a name given to several other 8th Air Force bombers, endured until 28 March 1945, when it was lost over Berlin with Lt Edgar Price's crew. *Sleepy Time Gal* was written off after an accident. The red paintwork identified aircraft of the 1st Combat Bomb Wing and were the first bright markings seen on Fortresses for formation identity. (USAAF K2281)

▲ A three-plane 'vee' of 381st Bomb Group B-17Gs over a patchwork of East Anglian harvest fields, high summer 1944. The Fortress nearest the camera, named *Passaic Warrior*, survived hostilities, the lead aircraft was battle-damaged on 12 December 1944 and salvaged in liberated territory on the Continent, and the far aircraft went missing in action on 30 October 1944. The Mustang escort is *The Iowa Beaut*, flown by Lt Robert Hulderman of the 355th Fighter Group. (USAAF K2299)

▶ Alerted by the firing of two red flares, signifying wounded aboard, ambulance crews watch intently as a Fortress makes its approach to runway 17. The Dodge ambulances are parked at the entrance to hardstand No 11. The Stour valley is in the background. (USAAF K2196)

▼ Worn and weathered, *Princess Pat* soars over Belchamp, Essex, in July sunshine, 1944. Battle damage was the cause of the obvious wing panel and tail surface changes. The veteran B-17G was received by the 533rd Bomb Squadron on 13 January 1944 and had completed over 100 combat missions by mid-March 1945. On the 27th of that month, while on an evening practice flight, the aircraft caught fire. Although the crew escaped without injury from the ensuing crash-landing at Ridgewell, *Princess Pat* could not be saved. (USAAF)

ROKE MANOR
HAMPSHIRE • STATION 503

70 RCD

◄ Fifteen large country houses were taken over for use as Rest Homes for combat airmen. Roke Manor (70th Replacement Control Depot detachment), north-west of Romsey, was opened in April 1944 for officers and could accommodate up to 25 at one time. The house was close to Stanbridge Earls, the first 8th Air Force Rest Home, opened in January 1943. Most of the men received were part way through a combat tour and deemed in need of a week's rest and recuperation. As can be seen, lawns often went unmown in wartime Britain. The spaniel in the photograph (taken in April 1945) probably belonged to a member of the staff. (Arthur Fitch)

▲ B-24J 44-10547 in flight over England, with a P-51 skipping over the clouds nearby. Of interest are the anti-radar jamming 'Carpet' antennae under the forward fuselage. (Harold Gage)

▲ *Do Bunny*, a 713th Bomb Squadron B-24 with more than 60 missions to its credit, was one of four 448th Bomb Group aircraft shot down by Me 262 jets on 25 March 1945. (Harold Gage)

► *Jokers Wild* and the 448th Bomb Group pass below other B-24 formations manoeuvring for position in the bomber stream. (Harold Gage)

▼ Sky Markers two seconds after release by the 448th Bomb Group lead ship. (Harold Gage)

▼ 'Eggress [sic] U-Uncle' was the radio call-sign of the 713th Bomb Squadron B-24J in the foreground of this photograph. This Liberator, serial number 42-78491, was one of only eight built by the North American factory at Dallas, Texas, that are known to have served with the 8th Air Force. It was also one of the three of this small batch that survived hostilities. (Harold Gage)

► A dog with a special claim to fame. 1/Lt Robert C. Peterson, on Captain Hughes' B-24D *Avenger*, acquired a cocker spaniel in England. He often took his pet on local flights and even fitted it with an oxygen mask. The dog was smuggled aboard when the Liberator was sent down to Africa in July 1943 and is said to have been taken on the famous low-level mission to Ploesti. Rusty was duly smuggled back into England. The photograph was taken in the summer on the lawns of Daws Hill House, when Bob Peterson had finished a combat tour and was working at 8th Air Force Headquarters. (John R. Johnson)

▲ On 2 March 1944 B-24J 42-100295 'V' of the 68th Bomb Squadron was flying over south Norfolk when the engines started to cut out because of a fuel transfer fault starving all four engines. The pilot, Robert Rose, put the aircraft into a descent towards the nearest airfield, Thorpe Abbotts. Despite foggy conditions, Rose was successful in making the airfield for a dead-stick landing, but the left landing gear collapsed, severely damaging the wing and No 1 engine. An inspection revealed enough damage to the main spar and airframe to make repair uneconomical and the aircraft was duly declared salvage. Many of the components would later take to the air again as replacements on other Liberators. (100th BG Memorial Museum)

▲ The 339th Bomb Squadron's *Little Joe* is signalled off for another mission on runway 23. It became one of the few aircraft in the 96th Bomb Group to survive to fly more than 100 missions by the war's end. The chequered flying control trailer is surmounted by the usual B-17 nosepiece and has a similarly painted command car for towing to the head of the runway in use. This photograph was taken looking west, with the southernmost hangars of the Eccles air depot in the background (Mark Brown: Air Force Academy)

▼ Fortresses in 'cab rank' as they marshal for take-off on the main runway, 23: a view from the control tower looking north. Aircraft on the perimeter track are assigned to the 337th Bomb Squadron. In the foreground is *Round Trip Ticket* of the 339th Bomb Squadron waiting its turn to pull out on to the perimeter track; it has the 388th Bomb Group marking on the right wing, suggesting that it had previously served with that unit.

The dark blue nose band was a squadron identity marking for the 339th. This aircraft was written off after a crash-landing at Snetterton on 5 February 1945. (Mark Brown: Air Force Academy)

▲ A B-17G of the 337th Bomb Squadron rolls along the perimeter track in a view from beside the control tower looking west. The ambulance is drawn up alongside the airfield recognition square containing the letters 'SN' (an 'SN' was also incorporated in the lead-in lighting to the main runway). The 'beehive' structure on the right, a common feature near control towers, housed the psychrometers and thermometers for local humidity and temperature readings. (Mark Brown: Air Force Academy)

◄ 2/Lt Beety giving Lady Moe a morsal outside a Nissen hut in the 338th Bomb Squadron area. The jackass was acquired in North Africa after the famous Regensburg shuttle mission on 17 August 1943. Flown back to Snetterton Heath, the animal became the Squadron pet, making a nuisance of itself until succumbing to the English weather and having to be put down. (Eugene Blue)

▼ The 338th Bomb Squadron barracks area on Site 1, looking east along the access road with a group of men reading the Squadron notice board. A frosty day, around Christmas 1944. (Eugene Blue)

▲ Part of the 338th Bomb Squadron's aircraft dispersal area among the wheat stooks, August 1944. The camouflaged B-17G on hardstand 27, 42-37716, was later transferred to another group. The view is to the north-east, with the Norwich–Wymondham railway line out of the picture to the right. (Mark Brown: Air Force Academy)

◄ A winter scene at hardstand 25 or 26, looking north and cold enough for most hands to be in pockets. The crew in front of the nameless B-17G are 2/Lt William D. Beety, pilot; Col Raymond E. Haule, radio; Col Marninc Nesterud, gunner; Col William F. Coleman, gunner; S/Sgt Rudolph Kocelick, radio operator; Col Arthur J. Milmoc, gunner; and 2/Lt Henry J. Stravato, co-pilot. The yellow nose band identifies the 338th Bomb Squadron; the 337th had red and the 339th dark blue, while the 413th did not have a colour marking. However, these nose bands did not appear on many of the Group's aircraft so it would seem that the practice was not fully adopted. (Eugene Blue)

▲ The Beety crew about to board *Five Grand* on a February morning in 1945. This Fortress was the 5000th produced by Boeing, who allowed its employees to autograph the aircraft before it left the factory airfield at Seattle. The hundreds of signatures covering the bomber drew interest wherever the aircraft visited. Despite a wheels-up landing, *Five Grand* completed 78 missions and was returned to the US in June 1945. (Eugene Blue)

▶ The freezing fog of the Christmas period 1944 produced an eye-catching spectacle, and one that will be remembered by many at this period – particularly in the bright moonlight, which made the English countryside look like a fairyland. Here navigator Lt Eugene Blue admires a hawthorn hung with hoar frost. (Eugene Blue)

▶ Amsterdam, the Netherlands, from the navigator's window of *Five Grand* during one of the food-dropping missions of early May 1945. (Eugene Blue)

▶ The stained glass window in Quidenham village church close to the Snetterton Heath living sites. The first group memorial in the UK, it was financed by the 96th's personnel and cost £600, which included the refurbishment of the chapel in which the window was placed. The Group emblem is in the apex panel and the four squadron emblems are in pairs at the top of each window. (Eugene Blue)

▶▶ *The Bad Penney* always did come back: a veteran of the great air battles of 1943, it became one of the few B-17F models in the 96th Group to survive combat. Pensioned off, it finished its days as a training aircraft used by Liberator crews of the 3rd Division to convert to Fortresses. (Arnold N. Delmonico)

▲ The control tower and signal square as seen from the perimeter track looking north. The vehicles with Alert Crews are the fire and rescue trucks. Red flags were intended to make taxying pilots more aware of camouflaged vehicles. An RAF Mosquito banks round in the distance. (Alexander C. Sloan)

► Capt. Glenn Miller's visit to Steeple Morden on 18 August 1944, when he and his band were flown in by two 466th Bomb Group Liberators. The famous band leader is here seen reaching inside his jacket for a cigarette. (Paul Chryst)

► The interior of a prefabricated hut that served as a barracks for personnel of the 1066th Signal Company. Various items of underclothing hang from ceiling lines to dry. The beds each have two 'biscuit' mattresses, which were, as one experienced soldier put it, 'the next best thing to sleeping on hard concrete'. (Alexander C. Sloan)

◄ A member of the 1181st Military Police Company in his corrugated iron sentry box at the main gate, situated on the south side of the Steeple Morden–Littlington road opposite the track leading to the HQ building and living site areas; this is a view looking east. The decorative pillar uses part of a 'drop tank'. (Alexander C. Sloan)

► The crew chief at work on Capt. Robert E. Woody's *Woody's Maytag*, probably trying to fix a cooling line; leaks were a frequent problem with the early Packard Merlin engines. Woody was one of the first fighter aces in the 354th Fighter Squadron, his total credits amounting to seven aircraft destroyed in the air and two on the ground. The air credits included four shared victories. (Alexander C. Sloan)

▲ S/Sgt Virgil Mcafee painting the *Man o' War* insignia on the 354th Fighter Squadron CO's P-51B in early April 1944. All Claiborne Kinnard's aircraft had this inscription and were, unusually, maintained by two brothers, Virgil and Darrell Mcafee, as crew chief and assistant crew chief. At the time they were aged 20 and 25 respectively. (Alexander C. Sloan)

▲ Another view of Maj. Kinnard's *Man o' War*, displaying a single victory, early April 1944. The 'bubble canopy', installed to give better rearward vision, was a British-made addition. Being in short supply, these initially went to squadron and flight commanders. (Alexander C. Sloan)

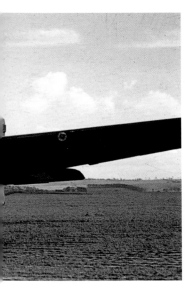

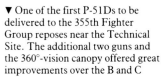

▼ One of the first P-51Ds to be delivered to the 355th Fighter Group reposes near the Technical Site. The additional two guns and the 360°-vision canopy offered great improvements over the B and C models. Even so, several pilots considered the earlier models faster and easier to handle. (Alexander C. Sloan)

▲ Capt. Stanley Silva in his P-51K, *My Catherine S*, leading a flight of 354th Fighter Squadron Mustangs high over East Anglia on 2 June 1945. The white letter 'C' on the top of some rudders indicates C Flight, often called Command Flight. A squadron was normally divided into four flights, A, B, C and D, for ground administration purposes. In the 355th Fighter Group only the 354th Fighter Squadron's C Flight consistently marked its aircraft. (Alexander C. Sloan)

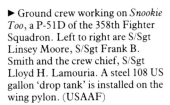

► Ground crew working on *Snookie Too*, a P-51D of the 358th Fighter Squadron. Left to right are S/Sgt Linsey Moore, S/Sgt Frank B. Smith and the crew chief, S/Sgt Lloyd H. Lamouria. A steel 108 US gallon 'drop tank' is installed on the wing pylon. (USAAF)

▲ When the 834th Bomb Squadron received its combat complement of Liberators shortly before leaving the US, the unit's commander approved a suggestion that twelve of the aircraft be named after signs of the Zodiac and Sgt Philip Brinkman, a former commercial artist, created some flamboyant art that was much admired. Unfortunately a few of these B-24Hs were soon transferred to other units in England, one or two before Brinkman had completed his work. The same design as on the transferred aircraft was to be applied to replacements but the attrition continued and eventually Brinkman abandoned the project. *Gemini* is here seen reposing on a hardstanding in front of No 2 hangar, May 1944. (Mark Brown: Air Force Academy)

◀ Resplendent in the 4th Combat Bomb Wing's yellow livery, the 833rd Bomb Squadron's *Short Arm* cavorts in the spring sunshine, 1945. This B-17G has the dark blue nose band identifying the unit, together with the call-letter 'A' (hidden by the wing in this view) in the same colour; part of the original painting of the letter (in black) can still be seen under the yellow fuselage bands. This aircraft was earlier assigned to the 835th Bomb Squadron and the propeller bosses retained the green colour markings of that unit. (Alexander C. Sloan)

▶ When the 486th Bomb Group converted to B-17s in July 1944 the identity marking was changed from 'O Square' to 'W Square'. These Fortresses were photographed from the top turret of another (the gun barrels can be seen on either side) while returning from a mission. The nearest, an 834th Bomb Squadron aircraft, has the propeller on No 2 engine feathered, but the Fortress reached home safely and survived the war. The further B-17G of the 835th Bomb Squadron, named *Wolfel Bear*, was not so fortunate and severe battle damage received during the mission on 10 November 1944 caused its pilot, Lt James Dimel, to make a crash-landing on the Continent. (Alfeo Brusetti)

▲ Without a farmer's presence, mayweed blooms unhindered on former agricultural land. Here shot up by fighters, B-17F *Raunchy* reposes in an undignified manner at the end of runway 28 on a bright August day in 1943. A flat tyre and bullet holes were easily repaired and this B-17F of the 351st Bomb Squadron was soon operational again though would fly no more than sixteen missions. On 6 September 1943, during a mission frustrated by weather, *Raunchy* was again attacked by fighters. His aircraft badly damaged and separated from the formation, Lt Sam Turner decided that there was little chance of returning safely to England and so headed for neutral Switzerland. A successful ditching was made on Lake Constance and all the crew members, except the ball turret gunner who had been killed in the air fight, were able to escape safely before the bomber sank. (100th BG Memorial Museum)

▼ Down among the buttercups: a Fortress about to land on the main runway (10) during the summer of 1944, viewed looking north-west with hardstand 1 and roadside cottages in the background. The main runway at Thorpe Abbotts was unusual in that it was 300 feet longer than those at most wartime bomber airfields built to Class A standard. (Mark Brown: Air Force Academy)

◄ Boldly marking their passage through the heavens, the high squadron of the 'Bloody Hundredth' forges ahead towards its target, March 1945. At this time the Group had a black diagonal wing stripe as an additional marking. (100th BG Memorial Museum)

▼ Crew members of *Lady Geraldine* put their feet back on 'Ol' England' and light up after returning from a mission, summer 1944. The 6 × 6 truck will take the crew to debriefing from hardstand No 38, situated to the west of hangar No 1. This view is to the south-east. This aircraft continued to bring her crews back safely for the rest of the war – she flew 75 sorties in all – and was returned to the US in May 1945. The original arrangement of the black feet silhouettes was deemed to be too suggestive by the authorities and was changed. (Mark Brown: Air Force Academy)

▲ A formation of 100th Bomb Group Fortresses on a mission in March 1945. The nearest is a 350th Bomb Squadron aircraft. All have the black-painted rudder marking introduced the previous November. (100th BG Memorial Museum)

► Trouble with No 2 engine during a flight caused the pilots to feather the propeller. Here, having removed the cowlings and done preparatory work, mechanics prepare to remove the propeller prior to the removal of the engine. Work is taking place on hardstanding No 32, looking north-east. (Mark Brown: Air Force Academy)

▲▼ Sixty missions and two enemy fighters destroyed is the claim recorded on the nose of *Our Gal Sal*, a 351st Bomb Squadron B-17, summer 1944. A 'lucky ship', she survived over a hundred combat missions to be returned to the US a year later. (Robert Astrella)

▲ *Fever Beaver*, the first B-17 in the 100th Bomb Group to complete 100 missions without an 'abort' (a turnback for mechanical or personnel reasons) went on to fly 125 by the war's end. It commenced combat with the 351st Bomb Squadron in January 1944 and was flown back to the US in the summer of 1945. Sgt John Pearson was the crew chief. (100th BG Memorial Museum)

▼ The proclaimed Irish ancestry of six members of his crew led Lt Mark Wilson to have the B-17 assigned to him named *Shilaylee*. The Fortress commenced operations in February 1944 and was a frequent recipient of battle damage. It endured for three months until, with a different crew, it failed to return from the Berlin mission of 24 May 1944. All baled out and were taken prisoner after

the B-17 was set on fire by fighter attack. (100th BG Memorial Museum)

▲ Named *Our Mark* by the original crew in December 1943, this B-17G was renamed by Lt Seymour Eichen when his crew took it over. *The All American Girl* endured for 98 missions, only to be lost on 10 January 1945 with 1/Lt John Dodrill and crew when Cologne

was the target. This aircraft was last seen disappearing into cloud with an engine feathered. Exactly what occurred is not known but it is assumed that the aircraft went into the sea with the loss of all aboard. John Dodrill was only 19 and was said to be the youngest first lieutenant in the 3rd Division. (100th BG Memorial Museum)

▲ The 351st Bomb Squadron's *Piccadilly Lilly II* flew 39 missions. On take-off for the next, problems were encountered. The pilot, Lt Paul Kohler, tried to stop the bomber's roll but ran off the end of the runway, crossed a road and a ditch and finished in a farmer's field. The aircraft was recovered and although it appeared undamaged a test flight showed it to be extremely difficult to control, indicating distortion of the airframe. As a result *Piccadilly Lilly II* was declared salvage on 27 June 1944. (100th BG Memorial Museum)

▼ Christmas 1944 was memorable for the hoar frost that coated everything with shimmering crystals and the trees in Billingford Wood made a spectacular backdrop to Fortresses of the 418th Bomb Squadron. This is a view past a frost-coated tail on hardstand 49, south-east to hardstand 47. The small hut is a toilet improvised from packing cases. (100th BG Memorial Museum)

▲ *Silver Dollar* was a popular name for aircraft received in natural metal finish. Thorpe Abbotts' Fortress of that name flew 106 missions with the 351st Bomb Squadron. Damaged in a taxying accident towards the end of hostilities, it was officially written off as salvage but in fact the aircraft was repaired and operated by the Group Headquarters as a 'hack' for several months after VE-Day – although officially it did not exist! The two hammer and sickle symbols are for shuttle missions to the USSR. (100th BG Memorial Museum)

◄ During an official visit by the Royal Family to 8th Air Force bases in the Bedford area on 6 July 1944, Princess Elizabeth 'christened' a B-17G named in her honour. *Princess Elizabeth* was proposed but did not meet with official approval so an alternative, *Rose of York*, was chosen. A bottle of champagne was suspended from the nose and a steel plate fixed between the chin turret gun cooling barrels to act as a breaker. After a bouquet of white roses was presented, the Princess posed for photographs with the 306th Bomb Group CO, Col Claude Putnam, before the christening ceremony. Assigned to the 367th Bomb Squadron, the aircraft was lost on its 63rd mission, the Berlin raid of 3 February 1945. Having sustained flak damage to two engines, the Fortress was last seen over the North Sea. Guy Byan, a senior BBC reporter on board, was lost with the rest of Lt Vernor F. Daley's crew. (USAAF K2163)

▲ *Lassie Come Home*, a long serving B-17G of the 367th Bomb Squadron, was badly damaged in August 1944 and again in January 1945. The replacement rudder shows some patching. The photograph was taken on hardstand No 20, looking east towards the hangar line, May 1945. (Ben Marcilonis)

▼ *Punchy*, the B-17G from which the aerial photographs in this section were taken. (Ben Marcilonis)

◄ This and the following four photographs are part of a series taken during a flight over southeast England early in May 1945. The photographer, Ben Marcilonis, a welder, was awarded the Legion of Merit in 1943 for his work in fabricating the nose gun mount that was adopted as standard on B-17s. Here one of the oldest Fortresses still operational at Thurleigh in May 1945, *Skipper*, shows its worn and faded camouflaged paint. Assigned to the 367th Bomb Squadron in February 1944, the bomber was severely damaged in November but after repair went on to complete over 100 missions. Note the bare metal replacement section and numerous 'silver' flak patches. (Ben Marcilonis)

▼ A 367th Bomb Squadron B-17G flying over Bedfordshire. The Squadron's aircraft were identified by red fin tips and propeller bosses. (Ben Marcilonis)

▲ Fortress 46604 is another bearing evidence of its war service; flak patches are to be seen on its tail. (Ben Marcilonis)

▶ The three groups of the 40th Combat Wing were the only ones in the 8th Air Force to carry the group letter identity marking on the undersurfaces of their B-17s' wings. (Ben Marcilonis)

▲ Another 367th Bomb Squadron B-17G of the formation, photographed as it passes over Benson airfield in Oxfordshire. The River Thames can be seen on the right. (Ben Marcilonis)

▶ Photographed at Harrington in May 1945, *Naughty Nancy* exhibits the blue propeller bosses that identified the 423rd Bomb Squadron within the 306th Bomb Group. The B-17G in the background is *Pretty Baby* of the 751st Bomb Squadron, 457th Bomb Group. (Air Force Academy: Mark Brown)

TIBENHAM

NORFOLK • STATION 124

▼ On 6 April 1945 a fairly new pathfinder B-24J, 44-48854 of the 445th Bomb Group, was on a training mission when it suffered an engine failure. The pilot made an approach to land at the nearest airfield, Thorpe Abbotts, but was warned off by flares from Flying Control when approaching a runway not in use. The Liberator appeared to start pulling away to make another approach but then either the pilot made the fatal mistake of turning into the dead engine or airspeed fell off to such an extent that the left wing dropped. In a matter of seconds the B-24 had turned on its side and plunged into a small wood near Thorpe Abbotts village. All on board were killed. (100th BG Memorial Museum)

WATTISHAM

SUFFOLK • STATION 377

479 FG

434/435/436 FS

► Sgt Fred Hayner modelled his superb painting for Lt Berkeley Hollister's P-51D *Pin Up Girl* on a Varga calendar painting (the same as used by the 490th Bomb Group artist for *Love 'Em All* – see under Eye). Hollister had two air victories to his credit while flying P-38s in August 1944. *Pin Up Girl* went down with another 434th Fighter Squadron pilot, Lt John C. Donnell, during an air battle near Berlin on 14 February 1945; Donnell had one air victory obtained the previous November. (Fred Hayner)

▼ The Mosquitos of the 25th Bomb Group (R) were employed in a variety of tasks where a fast two-place aircraft with a good payload was required. In late October 1944 the first of a score of Mosquitos was sent to the air depot at Abbots Ripton for the installation of chaff dispensing equipment. 'Chaff' was the code-name for the strips of metallic foil released to confuse enemy radars; although carried by the bombers, there was also a need for aircraft to fly ahead of the strike force to drop chaff with the aim of troubling the ground radars before the bombing began. This Mosquito XVI of the 653rd Bomb Squadron was one of the very first equipped for the task. The all-red tail surfaces were an identity marking applied as a result of 'friendly' fighters mistaking the type for the enemy Me 410 and attacking. (Robert Astrella)

▶ MM388 was one of the oldest Mosquitos at Watton when this photograph was taken in May 1945 – although later the same month the aircraft was written off following an accident. Red spinners identified aircraft of the 654th Bomb Squadron. Even allowing for some overexposure of the photograph, the blue finish is somewhat faded. (Air Force Museum)

▲ *Umbriago* was the PFF leader of the 392nd Bomb Group formation for the mission to bomb an ordnance plant at Kassel on 7 October 1944. On leaving the target area, this B-24J suffered hits from a nearby flak burst which wounded one man and disabled two engines. Successfully avoiding other flak areas, the pilot, Capt. O.B. Grettum, managed to nurse the bomber back to friendly territory to make a landing at Brussels/Melsbroek. The left landing gear folded soon after touch-down but no crew injuries were sustained. (RAF Museum)

WORMINGFORD

ESSEX • STATION 159

55 FG

38/338/343 FS

▲ A Mustang silhouetted against the setting winter sun: a view south-west from hardstand 38 on the north side of the airfield. (Robert Sand)

► Fortresses coming home from another mission pass over Wormingford: a view south from No 2 hangar apron across the perimeter track. The deserted house was used for storing hay, the occupants having been moved when the airfield was constructed. The building fell into disrepair and was eventually partly demolished by a crash-landing RAF Halifax. (Robert Sand)

▼ The still, frosty morning of 26 December 1944, looking north from hardstand 19. The black and white stripe-nosed P-51s of the 20th Fighter Group had been diverted to Wormingford because of bad weather and are parked among Mustangs of the 338th Fighter Squadron. The latter's pilots are in or near their cockpits awaiting 'cranking time'. (Robert Sand)

◄ Maj. John D. Landers' *Big Beautiful Doll* with an impressive victory display, photographed on 5 August 1944. The Japanese credits were obtained while flying P-40s with the 9th Fighter Squadron in the South-West Pacific Area during 1942. A second tour, in the ETO, saw Landers given command of the 38th Fighter Squadron and later the 357th and 78th Fighter Groups. At the end of the war his total victory tally was 14½ in air combat, the half being shared with another pilot. (Robert Sand)

▼ Fossil fuel was rationed but there was plenty of wood around. Here a bench has been procured locally and a Jeep jacked up on one side to enable the right-hand front wheel to be used for powering a saw – not a particularly safe practice but apparently effective! The location is near the mess hall. (Robert Sand)

▲ Line chief Sgt Robert L. Tudor running up P-38J 'CG:P' of the 38th Fighter Squadron on hardstand 29, 15 May 1944. With both turbo-superchargers cut in, the power blast blows up a dust cloud. The noise was considerable! (Robert Sand)

▼ Preparing for a post-war review on runway 05-27 with all the 55th Fighter Group's serviceable aircraft strength. The 38th Fighter Squadron is at the back (left in photograph), the 338th takes up the centre and the 343rd can just be glimpsed in the front line on the right. Some Mustangs had to be correctly positioned by tractor as a passing summer shower defeated manpower. The Jeep belongs to the 818th Air Engineer Squadron. The P-51 lettered 'CL:G' was *Little Trixie*, the personal mount of Lt Carroll D. Henry. (Robert Sand)

▲ Home-made wooden crew stands for working on aircraft repose amidst the slush of a snow thaw, January 1945. No flying today. (Robert Sand)

► Officers and enlisted men wait for transport into town near the main camp entrance MP guard point in the early evening of Wednesday 30 August 1944. Trucks left for local towns most nights of the week. (Robert Sand)

▲ On 21 May 1944 Lt Peter Dempsay of the 338th Fighter Squadron was strafing when he was confronted with a line of electricity pylons. With insufficient time to evade them, he attempted to fly under the cables but fouled two. Despite the damage to the P-38 he managed to retain control and nurse the aircraft back to a successful landing at base. (Robert Sand)

► Coffee and doughnuts, brought by Jeep and dispensed by a Red Cross girl to men working near the fuel dump in the bright morning of 12 April 1944. Refreshments provided by the American Red Cross came morning and afternoon to mechanics 'on the line' at most airfields. (Robert Sand)

► Many a damaged or troubled 8th Air Force aircraft put down on an airfield in a liberated area of the Continent when returning from operations. The 5th Strategic Air Depot was set up specifically to deal with these aircraft, its headquarters being established at Merville, whence detachments were placed at a number of airfields. The airfield outside Liège saw many 'lame ducks' land, most simply short of fuel. It also gave an opportunity for crews to answer the call of nature after long confinement at high altitude, which tended to disturb natural functions. Here the photographer took unfair advantage of some of Lt Beety's crew (Marvin Nesterud and Ray Haule) among the bomb rubble when their 96th Bomb Group B-17 put down on this former *Luftwaffe* airfield. The line-up of bombers, taken in the autumn of 1944, comprises 381st Bomb Group B-17 *My Son Bob*, the camouflaged 457th Bomb Group's *Mission Maid*, the 453rd Bomb Group's B-24 *Star Dust* and a Liberator from the 93rd Group. (Eugene Blue)

ON THE CONTINENT

GARDELEGEN

◄ In the final months of the war few if any airfields in Germany were safe from the ground-strafing forays of Allied fighters, predominantly the P-51s of the 8th Air Force. Gardelegen had been a target for both bombers and fighters. The burned-out wreck of a Focke Wulf Fw 190 is evident in this photograph taken on 14 April 1945 when the airfield was captured by ground forces. (Via Robert Sturges)

▶ Typical of the devastation wrought by Allied bombing at many cities and towns in Germany was the centre of Nürnberg in May 1945. Its rail marshalling yards and armoured vehicle factories were targets for 8th Air Force heavy bombers on four occasions, and also for RAF Bomber Command attacks. Inevitably many civilian properties and historic buildings were destroyed and damaged, the spire of the fourteenth century Church of Our Lady (in the centre of the photograph) being demolished. It was at Nürnberg that Adolf Hitler held his Nazi party's Annual Congress. (USAAF)

▶ Colour photography may have been comparatively rare during the Second World War but this and the following four colour pictures, taken at a prisoner of war camp in Germany, must be unique. On 11 December 1943 2/Lt Linn Stuckenbruck parachuted from a stricken 385th Bomb Group Fortress over Holland. He had his camera loaded and a 35mm Kodachrome film in his pocket. When he was captured the camera was taken and followed him to the Oberursel interrogation centre and then to Stalag Luft I, where it was kept in the *Luftwaffe* administration offices. The Germans could see that none of the film had been exposed and it was apparently of little interest to them, although someone had unsuccessfully tried to prise the camera open, letting in a little light which was to affect the colour process. When the *Luftwaffe* handed over the camp to the Allied

prisoners on 1 May 1945, Stuckenbruck found and retrieved his camera, and some of the pictures taken during the first few days of liberty at Stalag Luft I are shown here.

This view shows barracks huts in North 2 compound, looking north-west from a guard tower. The buildings were raised above ground level to enable guard dogs to search beneath for escape tunnels.

Excavations beside the huts are trenches dug as air raid precautions at the end of the war in case the camp was mistakenly attacked by Allied aircraft after the Germans departed. (Linn C. Stuckenbruck)

► A typical guard tower in which *Luftwaffe* personnel were constantly on duty during PoW occupation of the camp. This one was on the inner division bordering South compound and overlooked the shower block, parade area and solitary confinement cooler. Barth church can be seen in the distance under the tower steps. (Linn C. Stuckenbruck)

▼ Spring's first warmth raises vapour from the last of winter's ice. The snow has been compacted by the feet of hundreds of prisoners walking round North 2 compound beside the warning wire which they were supposed not to touch. The space between the double perimeter fence was filled with compressed barbed wire. The photograph was taken from a guard tower looking south at North 1 compound, early May 1945. (Linn C. Stuckenbruck)

▲ The Soviet army commander arranged for a troop of Russian performers to entertain the liberated inmates of Stalag Luft 1 with songs and dances. Among the audience were several Red Army officers, seen here to the right of the red-bereted British 1st Airborne Army soldiers. (Linn C. Stuckenbruck)

► Fish caught in the Baltic inlet to the west of Stalag Luft I provided a welcome addition to the contents of Red Cross food parcels, which were the basis of the ex-prisoners' meals in the days immediately after liberation. Here Lt Marion Wiles and Lt Bill Nicholls clean their catches ready for the pan. (Linn C. Stuckenbruck)

▲ Homeward bound. Between 19 May and 9 July 1945 a total of 2,118 B-17s, from 31 bomb groups and carrying 41,500 men, were redeployed to the United States; this represented the main body of the 8th Air Force bomber force. Aircraft of the remaining nine groups were gradually withdrawn over the next year by various routes across the North Atlantic. (Arthur Fitch)

▼ Kingman, Arizona. Awaiting the breakers: hundreds of 8th Air Force Fortresses – with some from the 15th Air Force – parked in the desert. The photograph was taken from the adjacent rail line in 1946. The sun has already partly faded the colourful markings on many machines. In the foreground are B-17s 'M' and 'C' of the 447th Bomb Group, 44-8310 and 43-38466 respectively; the latter's wartime service had been with the 379th Bomb Group (it retains that unit's device on the right wing). The 351st Bomb Group's *Silver Dollar* is the aircraft in the right foreground, a veteran of 121 combat missions. Directly beyond, in the next row, is the 452nd Bomb Group's *Hi Blower*. Fortresses that served with at least fifteen different groups can be seen in this picture. (Byron E Trent)

▲ A year later *Hi-Blower* had been moved into the forward ranks of the multitude, still simmering in the desert heat. B-17s sporting the fading colours of the 490th, 91st, 95th, 447th, 487th Bomb Groups, as well as of the 301st and 483rd Bomb Groups of the 15th Air Force, can be seen in the front two rows, and those of most other 8th Air Force Fortress-equipped units in the rows beyond. In the distance, towards the Peacock Mountains, are similar rows of B-24 Liberators. Now all that remains on this wide, arid plain is the sage brush. (Jerry McLain)

▶ *Stage Door Canteen*, 'christened' by actress Vivien Leigh at Ridgewell on 21 April 1944, awaits its fate in the Kingman desert. This 381st Bomb Group veteran completed 125 missions. (Via Dave Osborne)

INDEX

INDEX OF PLACE NAMES

INDEX OF AIRCRAFT NAMES

INDEX

INDEX OF PERSONNEL

▼ Sunset at Kimbolton, March 1944. (Edmund H. Lutz)